S0-AWG-223

Also by Steven E

1994
Wake Up
An Inspirational Handbook

2001
Wake Up...Live the Life You Love
(First Edition)

2002
Wake Up...Live the Life You Love
(Second Edition)

2003
Wake Up...Shape Up...Live the Life You Love

2003
Wake Up...Live the Life You Love: Inspirational How-to Stories

2004
Wake Up...Live the Life You Love In Beauty

2004
Wake Up...Live the Life You Love, Living on Purpose

2004
Wake Up...Live the Life You Love, Finding Your Life's Passion

Coming Soon
Wake Up...Live the Life You Love, Finding Personal Freedom

Wake Up...Live the Life You Love,

Wake Up Life the Life You Love,
Purpose, Passion, Abundance

By Steven E and Lee Beard
And 40 inspirational coauthors

Wake Up...Live the Life You Love,

Published by:
Little Seed Publishing, LLC.
P.O. Box 4483
Laguna Beach, CA 92652

Pre-Press Management by TAE Marketing Consultations
Robert Valentine, Senior Editor; Erin Forte, Editorial Coordinator;
Adam Mathis, Assistant Editor;
JP Crawford, Editorial Assistant
Text Design: Klansee Bell

Cover Illustrations: Klansee Bell

Distributed by Seven Locks Press
3100 W. Warner Ave. #8
Santa Ana, CA 92704

Library of Congress Cataloguing-In-Publication Data
ISBN: 0-9644706-8-3

$14.95 USA   **$24.95 Canada**

Dedication

As we travel down our chosen paths,
Many people we will meet.
Who stays and who goes?
Things that we will never know –
Until a bond is formed that cannot be broken.
The bond that guides us to our purpose.

People can be found anywhere we go,
But it is only at special times
When we can find one to carry us throughout our life.
When we find that special bond, never should we let it go
This bond creates a best friend and then we know –
Our purpose is our passion.

Not everyone in your path will agree,
Follow your heart - one day, they'll see,
A dedication stronger than any and every before.
A dedication that carries through broken times,
Allowing the dream to be in view,
Your purpose, your passion, your abundance of life.

To the purpose and passion of our authors,
may your life be full and abundant.

Steven E and Lee

How would you like to be in the next book
with a fabulous group of best-selling authors?
Another *Wake Up* book is coming soon!

Visit:
WakeUpLive.com

Additional author information can be found at:

We would like to provide you with a **free**
gift to enhance this book experience.
For your free gift, please visit:
WakeUpGift.com

Contents

Mark Victor Hansen 1
101 Goals

Martin Brown 3
Giving is Receiving

Wayne Dyer 5
Embrace Silence

Deepak Chopra 7
Why Am I Here?

Emily Jane Slater 9
Joseph's Angel

Kevin Nations 11
The Power of Decision

Steve Karagiannis 13
The Smile That Makes Your Knees Buckle

Bill Harris 15
Consciously Aware

Dr. R. Winn Henderson 19
People Are Starving

Laurelle Gaia 21
The Power of Spiritual Healing

Elaine Blom 23
A Reason to Be

Jim Stewart 25
  Value Your Vision

Jase Sounder 27
  Tiger Stripes

Jim Bourassa 29
  Born Again

Edward DuCoin 31
  You Can

Lyne Simons 35
  Love Yourself Enough to Live a Healthy Life

Jane MacAllister Dukes 39
  Being True

Dean T. Odmark...41
  Healing Power

Rex Johnson 43
  Designing Our Destiny

T. Harv Eker 47
  Your Money Blueprint

Matt Bacak 49
  Unleash the Powerful Promoter Within

Renee McLaughlin...51
  Change Your Script – Change Your Life!

Gregory Scott Reid...53
  Breaking Silence

Suzanne Balen...55
  I am mad. Are You?

Leigh Builder 59
  A Day in April

Brian Yui 61
  Taking the Plunge

JoeDee Seneker................................63
  Making Time

Sharan Ro 65
  Paradise Within – Living Aloha Wherever You Are

Steve Burgess 69
  At Dusk

Julie Dittmar 71
  Tummy Tickles and Two-by-Fours

Evelina Darlington 73
  Mind Power

Brent Gregory 75
  The Perfect Day

Pamela Harper................................79
  Dream Your Life Away

Martin Wales................................81
  Imagination Ignites Your Abundance

Jamie Hope 83
  S.T.A.Y

David Francis 85
  The Misfit Tree

Cynthia Chu 87
   The Blessing to Give Back

Alex Ngheim...89
   Take the First Step

Kay Snow Davis...91
   In Service to the Children

Steven E 93
   Visualization

Lee Beard..95
   The Big Ship and the Tug Boat!

Introduction

A Life Full of Abundance.

When we find the path that leads us to our purpose, we know we have found the passion that will fill our lives. It is this passion that fills our lives with abundance.

Abundance is something our authors have found. They fought through struggles, heartaches and conflicts; they have overcome hard times to find their purpose. They know the passion that can fill their lives. They have learned abundance in life can only be found in purpose and passion.

Abundance is having joy, excitement, love, the freedom to live your "perfect day."

It is living the life that you love – a life that brings meaning to others. Abundance is looking in the eyes of someone you have helped, knowing their "thank you" is the most important thing at that moment.

It is abundance that our authors have found. This book is full of inspirational stories by those who have found their purpose, passion, and are now living an abundance-filled life.

You have helped us in part of our purpose by just picking up this book. Let us guide you to finding your passion and your abundant life.

— Steven E and Lee

101 Goals
Mark Victor Hansen

Setting goals is one of the most important things you can do to guarantee your personal, professional and financial success. Goals are like a road map to your target destination. Each goal accomplished is another mile behind you on the road to your desire objective.

Most of us set goals in one form or another. But most of the time, we do not ask for enough, "I want to have a great job; I want my marriage to be successful; I want to have a million dollars."

These are goals for those who dip a toe into what they really want, but they are afraid to jump into the water. It is time to stop tip-toeing around the pool and jump into the deep-end head-first. It is time to think big, want more and achieve it all!

One of my favorite life-changing assignments is to have people write down 101 goals for themselves. This helps create a solid list of what they want to achieve in their lifetime. Then, after the initial list has been written, I ask them to create 10 outrageous goals by adding to their initial goals. These are things so extraordinary that 10 goals are all they need.

Why should people have 10 crazy goals? In order to come up with 10 outrageous goals, you must think outrageously. You must expand your mind and your realm of what is possible.

The bigger you think, the bigger your world becomes. You begin to think outside of yourself. The more you think outside of yourself, the more you begin to think and do for others. The more you do for others, the more rewards and benefits come back to you. It is a cycle that works for the betterment of both you and the world.

I believe, "Big goals get big results. No goals get no results or someone else's results."

— Mark Victor Hansen

Giving Is Receiving
Dr. Martin J. Brown

The gratitude of a worker returned to productivity following a severe back attack, the excited words of appreciation from a homemaker basking in the relief from long-standing headache pain, the joy in a child's eyes, no longer a bed-wetter, these represent only a handful of the multitudes healed naturally with chiropractic care.

My chosen profession provides improved mobility, relief from pain and suffering and enhanced quality of life for my patients. I am devoted to service, helping people thus improving the world. This is my primary purpose in life.

Service to humanity makes the world a better place, but service also makes me a better person. Giving to others strengthens me, and I believe in doing my small part to make this world a better place. I plant seeds now for another's future harvest. Life is good, and it is meant to be enjoyed. Make the most of each day and appreciate the goodness.

My Rotary service club works to raise funds for community projects, both locally and internationally. Our motto is "Service Above Self."

Of many worthy projects, we host a school-wide assembly for our county's emotionally impaired and autistic children. At this annual Valentine's event, our club caters a special lunch for all students and staff. We compose lyrics celebrating their school and sing them to popular melodies to the audience's delight. Each of our club members introduces himself at the microphone, sharing a few words of welcome and wisdom. The kids' highlight is our presentation of customized wrapped gifts to each student, such as a popular team sweatshirt. They are thrilled, and it is shown in their eyes.

The entire school buzzes with anticipation for days before this big event. The students eagerly await this annual recognition. The excited grin of one particular emotionally impaired little girl entering the gym with her class was infectious. Our club members, in their serving aprons, tearfully smiled. This child beamed proudly pointing to her gift sweatshirt from the last year. She recognized me from the prior year's event, and she ran up to me with open arms for a big cuddly hug.

That greeting really said it all. One young child's loving hug depicts the joy of life and my love of giving. Giving truly is receiving. Giving allows us to enrich others' lives – achieving our purpose as human beings, keeping our passions alive and filling our own life with abundance.

— Dr. Martin J. Brown

Embrace Silence
Dr. Wayne Dyer

You live in a noisy world, constantly bombarded with loud music, sirens, construction equipment, jet airplanes, rumbling trucks, leaf blowers, lawn mowers and tree cutters. These manmade, unnatural sounds invade your sense and keep silence at bay.

In fact, you've been raised in a culture that not only eschews silence, but is terrified of it. The car radio must always be on, and any pause in conversation is a moment of embarrassment that most people quickly fill with chatter. For many, being alone in silence is pure torture.

The famous scientist Blaise Pascal observed, "All man's miseries derive from not being able to sit quietly in a room alone."

With practice, you can become aware that there's a momentary silence in the space between your thoughts. In this silent space, you'll find the peace that you crave in your daily life. You'll never know that peace if you have no spaces between your thoughts.

The average person is said to have 60,000 separate thoughts daily. With so many thoughts, there are almost no gaps. If you could reduce that number by half, you would open up an entire world of possibilities for yourself. For it is when you merge in the silence, and become one with it, that you reconnect to your source and know the peacefulness that some call God. It is stated beautifully in Psalms, "Be still and know that I am God." The key words are "still" and "know."

"Still" actually means "silence." Mother Teresa described the silence and its relationship to God by saying, "God is the friend of Silence. See how nature (trees, grass) grows in silence; see the stars, the moon and the sun—how they move in silence. We need silence to be able to touch souls." This includes your soul.

It's really the space between the notes that makes the music you enjoy so much. Without the spaces, all you would have is one continuous, noisy note. Everything that's created comes out of silence. Your thoughts emerge from the nothingness of silence. Your words come out of this void. Your very essence emerged from emptiness.

All creativity requires some stillness. Your sense of inner peace depends on spending some of your life energy in silence to recharge your batteries, remove tension and anxiety, thus reacquainting you with the joy of knowing God and feeling closer to all of humanity. Silence reduces fatigue and allows you to experience your own creative juices.

The second word in the Old Testament observation, "know," refers to making your personal and conscious contact with God. To know God is to banish doubt and become independent of others' definitions and descriptions of God. Instead, you have your own personal knowing. And, as Meville reminded us so poignantly, "God's one and only voice is silence."

— Dr. Wayne Dyer

Why Am I Here?
Deepak Chopra

From an Interview with Dr. R. Winn Henderson:

The majority of people on earth are unfulfilled or unhappy because they do not have a purpose or a mission. As a part of the human species, we seek purpose and meaning; we laugh, and we are aware of our mortality (that one day we will die). This is what distinguishes us from other creatures. Laugher, mortality are purpose become three important, crucial questions. We search for meaning – a deep significance to life.

Why am I here? Why have I been placed on the earth? We've been placed on earth to make a difference in life itself and in others' lives. In order to make a difference, we must find what we are good at, like to do, and benefits others.

We all have a mission, and my mission in life is to understand and explore consciousness and it various expression and also to share that with anyone who's interested in doing the same. It boils down to understanding the mechanics of healing, the rule of love. I would say to put it very simply, my mission is to love, to heal, to serve and to begin the process of transforming both for myself and for those that I come in contact with.

As part of my mission, I founded The Chopra Center. My mission: to educate health professionals, patients and the general public on the connection between the relationship of mind, body, and spirit and healing. I teach people how to find their inner-self (most people have lost touch with theirs). When we find our inner-self, we find the wisdom that our bodies can be wonderful pharmacies – creating wonderful drugs – you name it, the human body can make it in the right does, at the right time, for the right organ without side effects.

The body is a network of communication. Our thoughts influence everything that happens in our body. The problem is many people automatically assume, "All I have to do is think positively, and everything will be fine." Because many assume this, they become unnatural and pretend everything is okay.

One must go beyond that; one must experience silence. It is when one experiences silence healing energies become involved and a balance is created. Psalms 46:10 says, "Be still and know that I am God." When the body is silent, it knows how to repair itself.

Pursuing my mission gives me fulfillment. It makes me whole. It makes me feel that I will continue to do what I have been doing. If I had all the time and money in the world, this is what I would choose to do. It gives me joy and a connection to the creative bar of the universe. I have realized that the pursuit of my goals is the progressive expansion of happiness.

Pursue your goals and find your happiness, wholeness, and balance in this world.

— Deepak Chopra, M.D.

Joseph's Angel
Emily Jane Slater

I am blessed to be Mother to twin boys, Joseph and Oliver. In his second year, Oliver died due to medical negligence. My sorrow was deepened to discover Oliver was part of a huge organ retention scandal, leading to his exhumation and the need to rebury him four times.

I was horrified when forced to look at his 'dead' organs in the mortuary. The nightmare continued when, because of a mix up, I had to again visit the mortuary to collect his testicles, handed to me in a cheap, open, cardboard box. His tongue was cut out and lost (possibly sold in Turkey).

Lack of compassion engulfed me. This was my child, the son I love dearly. When despair had completely overwhelmed me and I was weary and bruised to the bone, something miraculous occurred that changed my life forever.

Somehow, I touched the hand of the God that we are and was given a glimpse of a non-physical realm. I was shown that life, in its millions and trillions of forms, is eternal; death is nothing but illusion – the cosmic jest! Life wasn't meant to be a struggle. It was meant for living, laughing and loving in every moment, and we get to choose how we want our world to be. What we feel internally mirrors what we believe is reality. A magnificent entity showed many truths: life, death, spirituality, evolution and much more. These truths show us how to access an infinite field of intelligence. He refers to it as the mind of God describing the precise manner in which to utilize a power, to have the joyous life that is our birthright.

From the portion of consciousness, where Oliver now exists, he brings teachings and perspectives to our world. He calls himself Joseph's Angel to honor his twin brother, a love shared eternally.

One aspect of Oliver's teachings brings a lifetime gift to children. Joseph's Angel shows parents a process of how to teach children to read effortlessly. It is a consciousness based approach accessing knowledge within by applying ancient techniques accelerating reading ages by up to 6 years. Joseph's Angel opens the flow of wisdom for parent and child.

My sorrow was eased knowing the essence of Oliver is still here, still inspiring, making a difference, and he has much more to do! I self published Josephs Angel with enormous success. The world wants to hear Oliver and has his magic, his love.

Yes, I am blessed with two special boys, one for Heaven and one for Earth. I am able to pick up the pieces and be at peace as Oliver is. Now, I know the meaning of joy, and my cup runneth over.

Your own joy can be just a footstep away, or possibly a short walk. The distance is not important. You only require the intent. If someone had said to me, before the birth of Joseph and Oliver, "Do you want a lifetime of struggle or would you prefer joy?" I kid you not, I would have truly hesitated. Does that seem odd? Perhaps, because the selfimposed castle walls of attitude, seemingly get their own way. They seem to kick and shout, "We don't want to change. Let others change first!"

So, what are we to do? A joyful life would be more rewarding, more fulfilling, and so much easier than a lifetime of struggle. Yet, knowing this and being ready to welcome it is like climbing a mountain. The first step can lead you to your birthright to live in joy regardless of what others think or say, regardless of your own castle walls, old beliefs or old attitudes.

Have courage, intention and resolve. Grab the attention of your own inner guidance, and shout out, "Yes, I am ready, I have had enough! I'm living my life in joy, and I don't give two hoots what my inner or outer critics say!"

Wow! Yes, it feels so good to be alive.

Oliver, you taught me well. Loving you today, as always,
Your Mummy,

The moon will rise,
The sun will set,
But I won't forget'

— Emily Jane Slater

The Power of Decision
Kevin Nations

The Latin root for the word "decision" means "to cut off" or "to cut away from." If you are living the life you love or if you dream of that life, it will be the result of your decisions.

When you decide to possess, to pursue, to conquer or to enjoy life more fully, you're deciding to cut off the things that don't further those goals. You already have everything you need to reach your dreams, but sometimes the greatness in you isn't revealed until you decide to abandon those things that keep it hidden.

I am now much more aware of what it means to "decide." When I decide to accomplish a task, I know that there will be opportunities to prioritize things over completing the task. However, I don't have feelings of "I can't do that." Rather, I realize I have willingly limited my options to reach my pre-determined goal.

In his letter to the Corinthians, the Apostle Paul wrote, "When I was a child, I talked like a child; I thought like a child, I reasoned like a child. When I became a man, I put childish ways behind me."

How about you? Have you planned to start a successful business? Have you fantasized about speaking in public, about writing a book, about volunteering at a non-profit? Are you "putting off" those things which are contrary to your goals? Your highest contribution to the world will never be revealed until you give up your "right" to be mediocre. Your success hinges not upon your ability to acquire more, but to release that which hinders your success.

When Michelangelo sat down to sculpt "David," every attribute of that masterpiece was already enclosed in the block of marble he chose. What made "David" a masterpiece was

Michelangelo's ability to cut away precisely those things that did not reflect the final work of art.

In the same fashion, the value of a diamond is directly related to the talent of the diamond-cutter to precisely cut away that which hinders the expression of brilliance. Each cut is a balancing act between reducing the weight and maximizing the beauty.

Each day, as I make my decisions to live the life I love, I challenge myself to make wise decisions. However, I realize that the value of my future is shaped by the things I give up that don't further my goals. I can try to hold on to them, because they may seem like losses in the short run, but no masterpiece can be formed from my life if I resist letting go of that which prevents my true talents from being revealed.

My wish for you is the courage to live the life you love through the power of your own decisions. When you let go of those things that cover up your brilliance, your "safety net," you will reveal the masterpiece that is your life!

— Kevin Nations

The Smile That Makes Your Knees Buckle
Dr. Steve Karagiannis

I was having lunch with a friend of mine, and she mentioned she had become frustrated with her life. I was curious because she appeared to have everything going for her. She was in excellent health, attractive, bubbly and vibrant. She had that alluring level of confidence that attracts people. She had a well-paid marketing job with plenty of travel and recreational perks.

Naturally, I was curious. When I asked her why she felt this way, she slumped and told me that she wasn't enjoying her work and hadn't been for well over a year. She explained that her job wasn't satisfying anymore because she felt that there wasn't any real purpose to her role, other than creating profit for her company. She found the company's corporate culture of the company was profit-oriented and not people-oriented, which was incongruous, with who she wanted to be. Sighing, she admitted that she felt that her life had no meaning.

I was reminded of a story. "I'm not sure who wrote it, but it goes something like this," I said.

A man was walking along a construction site, and he saw a worker who was laying bricks. And he asked the man:

"What are you doing?"

"I'm laying bricks," he replied, "For a measly $10 an hour. Can you believe it?"

The man kept walking and he encountered another man who was also laying bricks.

"What are you doing?" he asked

"I'm building a wall" the second man replied.

The man kept walking and encountered a third man who was also laying bricks.

"What are you doing?" he asked

"I'm building a shelter for abused children" the bricklayer replied. "Can you help me?"

"Yeah, well, I feel like I'm laying bricks!" my friend exclaimed.

"Okay," I said, "what's something that inspires and motivates you in your life now?"

"My health. Helping others to become healthy. Making a difference to the world. But I don't want to lose the perks I'm used to now. I feel like I want to work in the area of health – perhaps education. I think that if I go down either of those paths I'll have to give up some of the things I've earned it."

"It sounds like you may have created a dilemma for yourself. You want to follow your heart, but you're concerned you won't be rewarded financially. Well, is it possible for someone to work in the area of health or education and to be rewarded the way you are?"

"I guess so," she admitted.

"So are you afraid you won't be rewarded, or don't you know of a job that would do that?"

"I guess it's the latter," she replied.

"And if you don't know, does that mean it doesn't exist?"

"No. It just means I don't know about it, yet."

"So what could you do?" I asked.

"I could look for one. I could search on the Internet, I could ask around. I'm in marketing for God's sake! If there is one, I can find it."

And just like that, her energy was back.

Later, as we were leaving she said, "It's funny. I'm still not 100 percent clear about my purpose. But knowing what is important to me makes me believe I'll be able to find out. If I'm working in an environment that's true to what's important to me then I'm at peace. And I can give myself the space to find out what I'm really here for."

"And maybe our purpose is to be true to our values," I added, "and ask ourselves how we can contribute to others in the biggest way we can. Maybe if we ask it consistently, we'll find the answer."

She smiled the smile that makes knees buckle, and we left.

— Dr. Steve Karagiannis

Consciously Aware
Bill Harris

Up until about age 40, I was definitely not living the life I loved. I was chronically angry, often depressed and had one abysmal relationship after another. I had no real career and no idea how to create one. The direction of my life was down or, at best, sideways.

This was a blessing in disguise, though because it created an intense motivation to learn what happy, peaceful and successful people were doing that I was not.

Today, I'm married to a wonderful woman who really loves me. I make ten times what I used to fantasize about and I have a challenging career dong something I love.

What's more, my anger problem is gone and I haven't been depressed for even one minute in nearly fifteen years. Now, at age 54, I truly am living the life I love. This transformation happened because I discovered a few key principles that created tremendous positive change for me.

What are these secrets?

First, happy people acknowledge that they are creating their realities. They see circumstances as influential, but know that what they do inside creates how they feel and behave, and what people and situations they draw to themselves.

For most people, this processing of external circumstances happens unconsciously. This makes it seem as if circumstances cause your feelings, behavior and what you attract into your life. When this happens, it seems as if you are at the effect of external causes over which you have no control. You feel like a puppet.

Happy people, however, even if they can't see how they're creating what is happening, know that they are. They take responsibility. Where the unhappy person sees what is necessary, or impossible, the happy person sees what is possible. By focusing makes those possibilities come true.

A third characteristic of happy, successful people is that they focus on what they want and keep their minds off of what they do not want.

Here's what I mean by focus. When you think, you make what psychologists call internal representations: pictures, sounds, feelings, smells, tastes or internal dialog. When you focus on something, you create an internal representation of it using one of these six methods.

These internal representations can be of what you want or of what you don't want. Take prosperity, for instance: You could focus on not being poor, or you could focus on being rich. That is, you could make a picture inside of poverty, wanting to move away from it, or you could create a picture of being wealthy, wanting to move toward it.

In both cases the intention is the same, but your subconscious doesn't care about your intention. It acknowledges the literal content of the picture. When you focus on riches, it thinks you want riches, and motivates you to see opportunities, find resources, and take action to be rich. When you focus on not being poor, it sees a picture of being poor, and motivates you to see opportunities, find resources and take action, but to remain poor.

Most people focus on what they want to avoid without realizing the consequences of doing so. When they get what they focused on, they assume they didn't focus hard enough and redouble their efforts. This creates even more of what they don't want, which creates more frustration.

The other penalty for focusing on what you don't want is that you feel bad. In fact, all bad feelings, and all negative outcomes, are the result of focusing on what you do not want.

Instead of unconsciously and automatically focusing on what you don't want, consciously and intentionally focus on what you do want. When you do this, you instantly begin to create it.

The final characteristic: happy people are consciously aware. As a result, their brains are less likely to run on automatic or create internal states and outcomes they did not intend.

How do you increase your conscious awareness? First: meditation. Second, investigate your own internal processes; your beliefs, values, ways of filtering information, strategies for decision-making, motivation and your other internal processes.

There is a price to pay to live the life you love. But paying it is a joyful enterprise and you will benefit for the rest of your life. Realize that you create your reality, learn to focus your mind on what you want and not on what you don't want, and increase your conscious awareness "First: through meditation" and self-inquiry.

The life you love is waiting for you!

— Bill Harris

People Are Starving
Dr. R. Winn Henderson, M.D.

Growing up during the early 60s, I wanted to share with the less fortunate in the world. I did this by donating money made by cutting the yard to help support and feed a little child from South America. By the time this child was old enough to be off the program, I, too, had grown up. Medical school, marriage and a new career consumed most of my time.

Through my medical practice, I donated time to treat those who had no insurance and no way to pay. This was now my way of giving to others. The plight of hunger had been put on hold. It is so easy to get caught up with our own lives that we completely forget about the people who need our help the most.

In my fifties, what seemed important in my thirties and forties no longer mattered. My focus came full circle to when I was as a grade school boy with a burning desire to help the hungry children in the world. God put this burden on my heart, and since then I have done everything within my power to do something about feeding these children. I wrote a book that explains how a person can take excess weight from his or her own body and transfer it to hungry or starving people in the world. No surgery is involved. Only a small mental sacrifice on our part is required.

Do we continue to fuel our bodies with food we don't really need, or do we use this asset to feed someone in the world who is hungry or even starving to death? When you think about it for just one second, the answer is clear.

We were not put here to constantly indulge ourselves. God fully expects each and every one of us to reach out to help the less fortunate.

Find out how I discovered this truth. I share my personal transformation on page 119 of *Wake Up And Live The Life You Love*, Inspirational How-to Stories.

If the TV commercials that picture starving families all over the world pull on your heart strings, please do something about these feelings. Hunger exists in every country including our own. This is not because hungry people are lazy, but simply due to the conditions under which these people were born. They simply have no money to buy food.

Feeding the hungry does not guarantee you a crown in heaven, but it will provide you with joy, happiness, and peace of mind. The most we can hope for when we reach Heaven is a pat on the back and to hear the words, "My child, well done!"

— R. Winn Henderson, M.D.

The Power of Spiritual Healing
Laurelle Shanti Gaia

O n some level, we all know that everyone has a birthright to be happy, healthy and prosperous.

When I was eight years old, I began to wonder what my life held in store, and then, my grandmother gave me a Bible as a gift. She said, "If you ever have any questions about life, all the answers are in this book." Enthusiastically, I began to scour the pages looking for my name, and the plan for my life.

Of course, I didn't find my name written, but I became mesmerized by the stories of Jesus' healings. I proudly announced to my family, "When I grow up, I am going to travel around the world, help people heal like Jesus did and teach them that they can do this, too."

The response was, "That's very nice, but you can't do that, only Jesus can."

"Oh, no," I said, "It says right here these things I do, you will do and even greater."

"I know that's what it says, but that's not what it means," was always the reply.

On that day, I had a conversation with God. I said, "God, I really want to help people like Jesus did. They say I can't, but the Bible says I can. So, I guess if I am supposed to do this, you'll help me."

From the moment I released that intention from my eight year old heart, and I was guided through good times and tough times. My grandfather's diagnosis with multiple sclerosis further fueled my desire to understand more about spiritual healing.

I spent many years in the corporate world until I was presented with the opportunity to put my dream into action. That was the day I was diagnosed with clinical depression as a result of corporate "burnout." I had allergic reactions to any medication the doctor prescribed. It was through my journey into deep, personal, spiritual healing, that I now live the life that eight-year-old dared to dream.

I have a soul knowing that all things are energy. Through my travels around the world, I have seen firsthand how prayer and Reiki (spiritual healing) can change the energy of a human being so much that radical chemo therapy treatments have little toxic effect. I have seen a broken bone set itself, and a burn heal before my eyes. I don't just believe in the power of spiritual energy to transform I know it to be so. I am convinced that we can utilize what we are learning about healing humans and apply it to raising the collective consciousness to awaken humanity to the promised "age of peace."

In my healing and teaching practice, I work with people who have a variety of chronic illnesses, like cancer, chronic fatigue, AIDS and fibromyalgia. Many people come to me for the simple aches and pains of everyday life, to relieve stress, and sometimes just to find a little serenity in a safe haven. Some clients desire a deeper connection with their inner guidance and awareness of their purpose in life.

I also serve as a healer for the California Pacific Medical Center's research project which is studying the effects of distance healing on quality of life for brain cancer patients.

We teach spiritual healing classes, produce spiritual books and guided visualization CDs which help our students and clients connect with their own inner healing power.

I now live in Sedona, Arizona, which was named the most beautiful place in America in USA Weekend. I am living heaven on earth.

Every morning I wake up and give thanks for Michael, the wonderful man with whom I share my life. Sharing a loving partnership with a kindred spirit is a blessing in itself, yet I smile every time I remember that we fell in love under the full moon on a black sand beach on the island of Hawaii.

I give thanks for the love Michael and I share, the healing work we do together, for our two beautiful children, for the infinite blessings in my life and for this opportunity to tell you that you are destined for great blessings in your life.

— Laurelle Shanti Gaia

A Reason to Be
Elaine Blom

It was close to five o'clock in the evening on April 16, 1994. I had no idea what time it was as I regained consciousness. I knew only that I could make out the faces of my beloved children standing at the foot of the bed. I couldn't speak because of the breathing tube in my throat. I couldn't move because they had tied me down so I couldn't pull out the tube in my throat or the multitude of IVs, tubes, catheters and central lines that were everywhere. Yet, it was such a precious moment, indelibly etched in my memory.

Sometimes, it seems it takes a scalpel, a few surgeons, myriad drugs and nurses and 101 staples for us to get the point. As awareness began to creep into my foggy, medicated brain, I lay in ICU overcome with an extreme gratitude. I felt (and still do) a connection to everyone.

Hours earlier, many highly skilled men and women carefully orchestrated the technical procedure of extracting my exhausted liver and replaced it with a lovely, healthy one from a person I never met, a gift from her family who I never met.

The skill of the surgeons would have been useless without the loving gift of these strangers. It isn't so much that I didn't know them; the amazing thing is they didn't know me. They didn't say, "Take this liver and give it to a single mother who teaches at a Midwestern university." They made the gift anonymously. In their heart of hearts, they wanted good to come out of their tragedy.

They wanted to share life, increase joy among humans, and make a positive difference, even if they would never have an inkling of the outcome. My two teenagers are now fine independent adults who have a mom to rejoice in their triumphs and listen to their woes. My daughter has an adorable two-year-old who would be missing a grandmother without this connection. Life is so rich, and I have so much more to give.

We are all connected. I don't mean by virtue of my having someone else's liver in my body; I mean by the virtue that we truly do want to live more, make a contribution to each other and that we are all breathed and moved by the same essence of life. We are here for each other.

If you are not now feeling that connection to others, my prayer is that you let my connection be your connection. It could have just as easily been you who got this gift. We are all part of the web of life. There are times in our lives when we don't feel loved or appreciated; we feel inadequate. It is tempting to believe that smallness is the truth of us. Yet you are so much more. We all need you and everything you bring to the world.

This could be just another story in just another operating room. Maybe, the point is every story is a story of connection. Perhaps we are so numb to the magnificence of life that we fail to notice the gift of each encounter, each event in our lives. Please don't believe the lie of the appearance of smallness, of separateness. You are very much needed and wanted in this world. Let the essence of you touch us all.

— Elaine Blom

Value Your Vision

Jim Stewart

It was five years ago when I noticed a hint of sparkling light in the corner of my right eye, but I didn't think much of it. I wrote it off as stress, a result of working long hours as the national sales manager for a company that was rolling out gambling machines countrywide.

It gradually got worse. Straight lines became wavy, and my eyes became extremely sensitive to sunlight – a bit hard to avoid when you live in Africa.

After a series of tests, I discovered that I had a form of macular degeneration at only 39. According to the specialists, this was more common in the 65 plus age group.

I went through the common stages that happen when a long-term illness strikes – denial, anger, depression, and then finally, acceptance. All my future plans were re-examined.

Now, I work for myself as a communications trainer and hypnotherapist. I am also building a career as a public speaker and Internet entrepreneur and, of course, an almost-famous co-author of the *Wake Up...Live the Life You Love* series.

One key to discovering and living the life you love is to spend time discovering what you value and how your current lifestyle fulfils those values. If it doesn't, ask, "What do I need to change?" Couple these values with a vision for your life and go for it!

Another key is to examine any limiting beliefs such as "I will never get better," "I can never be successful," "I'll never earn enough money." Get rid of them.

In deciding how you want to live your life, ask yourself, "If I won the lottery tomorrow, would I still be doing what I currently do?" If the answer is no, then you are halfway there. "What would I do?" is the next question. Once you answer these two questions, you can begin to work out your plan for how you are going to achieve what you really want out of life. A life that will make you happy and contented, the life we are all meant to experience.

A vision you value can keep you going when things get tough. A vision is not a dream, but a real "honest-to-God, energy filled, ambitious vision" fills you with happiness every time you achieve another step on the ladder to achieving it.

My current lifestyle allows me to spend quality time with my wife (and best friend), Sheila, and our friends. It also allows me to work when I choose and with whom I chose.

You know what I mean, don't you? Having to work everyday with people who are rude, angry, bored, depressed; just getting through the day working from one pay check to the next is tedious and draining. Now, I get to work with people who are excited, happy, optimistic, dreamers, doers and most of all, people I want to be around because they make me want to be a better person.

I discovered that you don't have to have a life full of material things to be happy. Nowadays, my central vision is gone in my right eye, and the left is deteriorating to the same point. I know that things will change even more in the next year or two. But do you know what? I'm looking forward to it (albeit a bit blurrily).

I am loving life more now than I have ever done before. And you can, too. It just takes vision.

— Jim Stewart

Tiger Stripes
Jase Sounder

Have you ever heard someone say "A tiger can't change its stripes?" This is usually stated when making the point about one's inability to change.

Well, it's not true. We can change anything about ourselves that we want to change.

What are our stripes anyway? Are our stripes our defining characteristics? Our physical body – hair, build, the color of our eyes, hair, skin? Who we are inside – confident or scared, dull or funny? Our social status? Whether we are single or married?

You can change all those stripes; you can change everything about yourself – giving yourself a complete makeover leaving room for an abundant life.

Why would someone want to change his or her stripes anyway? Here's why; life isn't going to change. If your life is not working the way you want it to, you have to change, and it is your responsibility to change the stripes that are not serving you.

This is true in all areas of your life except one – purpose.

To find your Purpose (with a capital P), forget for a while everything you have learned about which types of people become a success and what it takes to be a success. Instead of trying to fit yourself into a mold, get familiar with who you are already.

Figure out what stripes you have that are uniquely yours. Get to know and cultivate your stripes that are the boldest, most unique, most fun, and most natural for you. Your purpose is already within you, and when you begin to live a life based on your true self, your purpose will make itself known, and by default, you will fulfill it. As a bonus, the more you bring forth your true stripes, your life will be fulfilled with more ease, joy, and abundance.

— Jase Sounder

Born Again
Jim Bourassa

My parents emigrated from Canada, to join in the economic boom and raise a family. I am a first-generation American. When I was 2 years old, the Lord spared me from an often-fatal disease called spinal meningitis, a brain inflammation caused by a brain inflammation transmitted by a virus or bacteria. Because of the disease, I was "born again;" I had to relearn everything, including how to walk. The disease didn't damage my brain. I was later tested by my parents and was found to have the IQ of a genius.

My father was a top achiever and entrepreneur his whole life, and I inherited is drive. He taught me to set goals and strive to attain them. My mother gave me unconditional love and taught me to hold on to the Lord as my strength. Now, I am a very successful business owner, philanthropist, and inventor. When I was 15, I began a life-long project of learning about Aether (now called Dark Energy). I had three goals by that point: to improve upon Quantum Field Theory and Einstein's Relativity; to understand why we are here and what our role is in the universe; and, to be independently wealthy. About this time, I accepted Jesus Christ into my life, which gave me the belief that "I can do all things Christ who strengthens me!" (Philippians 4:13) In other words, I am supplied with everything essential to achieving the goal and purpose God has for me to bring Him glory.

I met my future business partner, the real estate mogul Francis "Frank" Sanchez, when I was searching for a home loan. He shared his real estate ideas with me, and we decided to create IFCFinancial, a dynamic real estate investment company that creates model homes from neglected and distressed houses. Later, I coined the registered trademark "InvestorTainment" as a combination of investment (think New York) and entertainment (think Hollywood).

As the business developed, Frank and I invented the Investor-DisclosureSystem™, a patent pending process that allows investors the ability to see how and where their money is being invested on a real-time, live basis. We have appeared on the cover of Crain's *Chicago Business*. General Alexander M. Haig, the Secretary of State for Ronald Regan, interviewed us on *World Business Review*. Terry Bradshaw interview us for the *"Pick of the Week"* show on MSNBC, which highlights companies like ours that represent the backbone of America's economy, are based on unique business models and reflect the best of corporate America.

I am also the Executive Director and Founder of Quantum AetherDynamics Institute. The Institute is an exciting new non-profit organization founded by David W. Thomson III and me to develop what we call the Aether Physics Model and to create new technologies based upon our research. Potential benefits of using the power of the Aether include generating pollution-free energy and promoting longer and healthier life.

My success story includes accepting nominations to prestigious organizations like the New York Academy of Sciences, developing relationships with global giants including Sir Arthur C. Clarke, author of *2001: A Space Odyssey*, and Robert Kiyosaki, international bestseller of *Rich Dad Poor Dad*. I have had dinner with powerful leaders including the President of the United States and the Lieutenant Governor of Illinois.

I sometimes wonder what would have happened if I had died when I was 2. How many lives will I touch before my time on Earth is over? There is power in one life, and the Lord has a plan for yours. That is why you are reading this now.

My philosophy for living a greater life is simple and easy to implement: Pray for guidance and write a life mission statement. Use it to create your daily plan. Then, step out and take the calculated risks necessary to achieve your goals, and never give up. Don't expect the world to give you anything, create your own opportunities. Don't let the jealousy and envy of people pull you down. You create your daily reality with your thoughts, your words, and your actions. Stay positive!

— Jim Bourassa

"You Can"
Edward DuCoin

I was an "only child" with five siblings. My two brothers and three sisters ranged from seven to twenty-one years older. Even though we are a very close family, I grew up during my teenage years as an "only child."

Because I had wonderful parents, I was never lonely. They spent their entire lives making sure we had everything we needed. My parents had things that money cannot buy – a loving family, friends, good health — the became wonderful grandparents.

However, my parents did not have many things that money could buy. When the three of us sat around the dinner table, I listened closely to what they said about money. I heard the stress in their voices and knew that, like most people, money affected their many dreams. They wanted to rent a motor home to travel across the county. I said, "Why rent it for two weeks? Buy one and have it whenever you want to get away." I was a smart kid but so naive about how tight the household money was.

My father worked odd jobs such as wallpaper hanging to bring in extra money. One day, when he did not know I was watching, I saw tears in his eyes as he lifted a ladder off the top of his car. Later, as he lay on the couch with a bag of ice on his left shoulder, he explained paper hanging inflamed his muscles. My dad did not want to work extra jobs in addition to his full-time position as a foreman, but it was something he had to do. He would be right back at it after church on Sunday.

The clues, hints and outright signs of money added up in my head like adding the final piece to a puzzle. We were not poor, but my parents' were limited by the consistent worry over money.

Two things happened that weekend as I watched my father. In a flash, I understood how great my parents are and what sacrifices they made to have six happy children. More importantly, I swore I would never let money be a barrier to my dreams.

As a college freshman, I made a commitment for success armed with the two gifts my parents ingrained in my head: "Respect for all who work hard to provide for others," (Dad) and the statement "You can achieve anything" (Mom).

Now, my daily ritual is to recite my goals and how I will achieve them. I always start with the words "You Can," just as my mom's statement did.

"You Can, get good enough grades at community college to transfer to a business school." I graduated from the Wharton School of Business three years later.

"You Can, start a business even though you have little money." I started a company in a spare bedroom with less that $200 that within ten years made the *Inc. 500* three years in a row as one of the fastest growing companies in the USA.

"You Can, take your company public." The company I started in my home went public on NASDAQ in 1999.

"You Can, become a race car driver." I got into my first racecar at the age of 33 and was so bad the instructor refunded my money. However, I stuck with it and raced in my first professional race a few years later.

"You Can, be a respected consultant and speaker." I now have the opportunity to speak worldwide and work directly with incredible business people.

"You Can, own a NASCAR Team." In 2004, Groove Motorsports was born and will race in the Craftsman Truck Series. We will race at the Nextel Cup Level within a few years because "We Can."

No achievement ever happens based solely on effort. I attribute my success to great people like my family, especially my brother (my business partner), the thousands of great employees I served and the belief that "I Can."

The most cherished moments in my life could not have been bought, such as playing catch with my son, watching my daughter make the game winning shot in basketball, and the feeling I had driving the final lap of my first professional race. However, I can say that living without my parents' financial worries offers me the resources to go after and obtain the life I love.

The only difference between those who achieve specific life goals and those who do not is the all-consuming belief that it can be done. You can do it, and I say will do it, only if and because, you believe it can be done. The "it" is anything. It is all there for you. You Can.

— Edward DuCoin

Love Yourself Enough to Live a Healthy Life
Lyne Simons

In 1989, I had received a blow to the head from a light fixture which fell two stories knocking me out while I was sitting in a seminar on a ship in Long Beach, California. I had a concussion, dizziness, tinnitus and short term memory problems. I was diagnosed with post traumatic stress syndrome and became very fearful and depressed. I began stuttering and forgetting my train of thought. I was later told I was very lucky I hadn't ended up in a coma or with any paralysis.

I thought my career as a speaker was over. I was forced to slow down, stop and be quiet for long periods of time. For the next 12 years, I lived a life of quiet desperation, trying to pretend all was as it used to be. My physical and emotional health on a fast downward spiral, I tried to pretend I was as good as ever, fooling no one but myself. At one point, my feelings of worthlessness were so bad, I attempted suicide.

Amazing how years of avoiding emotional issues can catch up with you in illness and stillness! I began a slow and often painful inward journey, searching for what my life's purpose might be, and why this had happened to me.

My turning point came when I heard how my friend, Carolyn Wunderlich, had turned her life around with a marvelous new system involving cleansing and good nutrition. She had been, diagnosed with a life threatening liver condition, which she was able to reverse without the recommended surgery, through this amazing method. When I first heard her courageous story, I was overweight, without energy, having joint pain and headaches. I couldn't wait to see what this cutting edge technology could do for me.

The immediate changes in my life were nothing short of miraculous! After 30 days, I was so enthusiastic about sharing it with friends and family, I overcame my embarrassment enough to reveal some really remarkable but very personal life changes. During my first 9 days, I had lost 12 pounds and 15 inches. I found this so remarkable I posted a before and after picture on my website. It didn't bother me to show the before picture, with my fat belly hanging over my swimsuit, because in the after I looked so different!

As I traded my poor eating habits for healthy ones, I started waking up each day with increased energy and vigor. What I didn't tell even some of my closest friends was that after 30 days on this marvelous new and easy nutritional system, I had secretly quit taking my depression medication and my hormone pills. Yet, I didn't have any more hot flashes or night sweats. My brain felt like a fog had been cleared out, and my memory began to work so much better.

My fear and depression are finally gone. I feel that I can handle whatever life sends my way without going to bed and pulling the covers over my head. After 12 years on anti-depressants, this alone has been life changing for me.

As a side benefit of cleansing my liver, my age spots have disappeared. My skin is softer and less wrinkled after hydrating my body with 64-ounces of water a day. After feeding my body with good nutrients, my hair is growing in thicker and shinier and my nails are growing long and healthy for the first time in 20 years! My 35-year addiction to coca-cola is over. I have no more cravings for candy, ice cream and chocolate.

Most remarkable to me is that as I shed the toxins from my body, I am also able to release those toxic emotions of self-loathing, anger, hatred and fear that I had stored in my heart and spirit for so long. I am healthier and look younger than I did 10 years ago.

I know now that millions of people with chronic illnesses, such as metabolic syndrome, can improve their quality of life with my system. Dr. Paul Berns, a Beverly Hills internist who specializes in integrative medicine and emphasizes good nutrition, supports my nutritional program. He states, "I have seen many patients lower their blood pressure, improve their lipid abnormalities and increase their general strength and vitality by a nutritional life style change."

There is an incredible lightness to my being now. At the risk of sounding overly dramatic, I feel as if I am now living more like what God intended when he created me. My body functions with grace and ease again and my spirit soars each day. I truly feel as if I have been released from a cage and am completely alive now. I have such joy and happiness when I wake up each day and feel such love for my new healthy self and for others. I am a woman with a mission, and it is no longer "mission impossible." I believe that I am now living part of my life's purpose when I tell others about this amazing Isagenix technology. I find I can be myself, love myself and even like the self I am!

Using this remarkable system has changed my body, mind, spirit and life! I love showing others how they can open their hearts, minds and bodies to good health and happiness.

In the universe of all time, You are the only you. Love yourself enough to be truly healthy and alive as you live a life you love!

— Lyne Simons

Being True
Jane MacAllister Dukes

My middle name is truth. My credo is speak true and be true – align yourself with your essence, and you cannot go wrong. Life is a living, wondrous, co-creative adventure. I can feel it pulsing through my veins as I write!

I always knew I had a greater purpose. I studied, read and followed my heart, if not always entirely trusting my instincts. Now, I know I knew more than I realized at the time. I was passionate, loving and generous, but I found it difficult to receive. I have since learned differently.

The big tragedies in my life included: my pony dying when I was 14; my father dying when I was 26; dealing with my sister's suicide when I was 37 and, at 42, miscarrying a baby boy at four months gestation. In between, there were smaller, less significant tragedies as well as joys, wonders and seriously sensational moments. I was moved by so much, and I knew that I was deeply loved, even if I could not explain why – though, sometimes I felt very alone – a kind of soul loneliness seemingly impossible to fill.

Each one of the awful, excruciatingly painful tragedies seared and opened me more and more, and each one bestowed great gifts upon me. Each of the "in-between" joys and wonders expanded my world as well. Life was filled with magic; I saw and felt God every-where. I could have done without the terrible pain, grief and loss, but I always knew there was a bigger picture, even if I couldn't see it at the time. Slowly but surely, I was opening to receive.

Now, I no longer feel alone. I love myself, this world and every-thing in it. I see more positive things than negative. I have moved from life happening to me to being life walking! I am a "lightworker." I am also an artist, creator, mother, lover, coach, cook, cleaner, chair-woman, company director, poet, singer, producer, coordinator, gardener, writer and probably a few other things as well.

The most important thing in my life is my family. My children, 13 and 7, are the delight of my life. It is an honor and a privilege to co-create our daily living with them and my extremely intelligent, well-disguised husband. I am lucky enough to have wonderful stepchildren, a fantastic mother who is still very much alive and kicking and three other unique and lovely siblings. I am also privileged to "work" in a profession that enables the realization of magnificent potential in others every day.

I have learned that spirituality does not require poverty. The joke is that when you surrender to all you can be, allowing yourself to keep becoming the best possible version of yourself, when you give yourself this gift, you also give them to all. It tickles me pink that when I evolve myself, I evolve all.

When I stand for truth, it is for everyone. In other words, when I selfishly pursue my own expanded conscious evolution, I am actually pursuing it for all.

Breakthrough experience facilitated by:

- Awakening your Lightbody and Divine Will series by Orinda Ben, www.luminessence.com,
- The Balancing Program – www.thebalanceprogram.com,
- David Cousins – www.soulspeaks.com and Soleira and Santari Green – www.SOULutions.co.uk
- Zoran Todorovich – and Ross McCullock D.C. (UK).

— Jane MacAllister Dukes

Healing Power
Dr. Dean T. Odmark

I've been a chiropractor for almost twenty years. My job has been to correct backs and eliminate pain. I strengthen nervous systems, get them up and running, and sometimes bring the almost dead back to life. But after many years of this kind of routine, I began to feel like a glorified back mechanic.

As a chiropractor, I could adjust up to 150 people in a single day. Some of those patients would have crippling arthritis, fibromyalgia or Irritable Bowel Syndrome. Some had severe allergies, psoriasis or deep depression. All of these people were coming to see me for their musculoskeletal problems like their neck pains, aching backs and frozen shoulders.

It was heartbreaking and frustrating for me to know that I was doing a great job helping these people with their aches and pains, but was inadequate to help them recover from serious and often debilitating disease. I felt powerless to give these people the quality of life I knew they deserved!

One of my deepest beliefs is the body is entirely capable of self-healing, no matter what the problem. Why was I seeing an increase of patients with auto-immune disorders and severe allergies? Drugs and surgery certainly did not appear to have the answers, and the medical profession seemed to be utterly baffled by these problems. Standard chiropractic treatment seemed to make only a minimal difference.

One day, while reading a booklet called The Healing Power of Herbs, I saw a small blurb on the last page about a controversial treatment called NeuroCranial Restructuring. Out of the blue, the author decided to throw in some personal experience with the NCR technique and how it had forever altered his life.

My interest quickened after I read those few sentences, but I immediately dismissed the idea. Interestingly enough, though, over the next few days my thoughts kept returning in an almost compulsive manner to those few words. To prevent total insanity, I acted.

I immediately researched NCR and discovered that there was going to be an intensive seven-day class the following week, limited to only six students. I agonized over whether I should attend or not. Would my patients accept this radical technique? Could I close down my business for an entire week to plunge into the unknown with so little notice? After a sleepless night, I called the next day to register and discovered that an opening had just become available that very morning.

I took a deep breath and made the decision to attend. My secretary had to call hundreds of patients to inform them that the office would be closed for an entire week. Rather than feel inconvenienced, my patients were excited. With their encouragement, I packed my bags, and I went into the adventure, feeling apprehensive but fueled by a deep certainty.

My NCR training was a one-of-a-kind experience. One of the most stressful weeks I've ever spent in my life, and also the most exhilarating. It not only changed my life, but the lives of my patients.

Since that time, I no longer worry about whether or not my patients will "accept" what I'm doing. I've found that what is of paramount importance is whether or not I accept it. If I trust that the universe is guiding me every step of the way, then jumping off that cliff gets easier and easier.

I'm no longer just a back mechanic. I'm still first and foremost a chiropractor, but I also successfully treat the symptoms associated with degenerative disease, auto-immune disorders, people who have suffered severe head injury, emotional problems, chronic allergies and life-destroying headaches. I'm privileged to have patients fly in to see me from England, Canada, South America, Mexico, and from other areas of the United States.

This never would have happened if I had not shoved myself out of my own duller-than-dull comfort zone. It's allowed me to live a life that I once thought was unattainable. I continue to listen to those inner urgings, and now welcome them rather than fear them.

— Dr. Dean T. Odmark

Designing Our Destiny
Rex Johnson

I spent many happy years growing up in South Africa. However, my mother died when I was 16 and I developed low self-esteem. When I started work, I mixed with "the wrong crowd" and drank excessively.

Then a hit-and-run accident left me virtually blind. In what seemed like an instant, I had lost most of my eyesight, my job, my ability to play football or drive, and my girlfriend had left me. I was devastated and suicidal.

While studying martial arts, a friend suggested that I attended a talk on personal development and "accessing your inner power." This talk was to dramatically influence my life. Continuing my martial arts achieved two black belts in separate styles of karate. As I couldn't get a job because of my visual problem, I opened a laundrette, and eventually owned two. While working there a young lady introduced me to meditation. This led to my studying homoeopathy with a wonderful teacher who introduced me to Holistic Health and many other great teachers and masters.

I went to natural therapeutic college and qualified in naturopathy, osteopathy, homoeopathy and herbal medicine. I gradually built one of the largest holistic health practices, treating 40 to 50 patients a day.

Finally, I felt that is was time for a change, so I relocated to the UK. Within a year, I had the largest holistic practice in Dorset. How was such a thing possible? Well, during my time in South Africa, I had developed my philosophy of Inner Power. We all have a power within us that created us, takes care of us and guides us every step of the way - if we are conscious of it and work with it. I have always taught it to my patients, and many have been able to dramatically transform their lives. My teacher always said that unless you attend to the consciousness of the patient, you are only removing symptoms on more subtle levels.

Then, in England, Jeannie became a patient. She had been ill for ten years and had been in hospital unable to walk. We both joined a group going to Brazil to see a famous healer, for I was quite desperate to regain my eyesight. During our last evening, we experienced an intense spiritual bond, and somehow knew that we would work and be together. Neither of us was looking for a partner at this time, and, although neither of us was healed in the way that we had hoped, we decided to work together. I always said that, though I had not regained my eyesight on my trip to Brazil, I had returned with complete vision.

Fortunately during this time, I had been working with a network marketing company specialising in nutritional and health products. They had proved effective with both myself and my patients, so I gave them to Jeannie. She gradually improved over a period of months and was soon back to full health and energy. We were both very impressed and, because of our mutual desire to help other people, we decided to start a business to spread the word.

It was during this time that we fell in love and now live in the beautiful countryside of Dorset. At our wedding, I expressed my gratitude to that Inner Power as I recalled how my damaged sight had led me to holistic healing, which led to my practice in the UK, which led to my wonderful friends and, almost inevitably, to Jeannie. This inner power is wiser that we are and plays a vital role in designing our destiny.

Because I have been helped by so many wonderful people, my dream is to help people to access their own inner power in order to achieve health, wealth, happiness and success in their own lives. To do this I have also qualified as a life coach and, together with my friend, Stephen Coburn, I have formed the "Inner Power Associates." We have formed the Bio-energetic Therapists' Association, teaching people how to help both themselves and others improve their health. We have also started a "Design Your Destiny" program aimed to help people to improve all aspects of their lives through personal development, with the option of qualifying as Holistic Life Coaches. Using these two programs, we have already helped many people dramatically improve their health and quality of life.

One lady came to me with cancer and was only given months to live. She chose to take the path of natural therapy. I treated her using the special nutritional health products. I taught her a range of techniques and strategies, and she also changed her diet. She also went on both our Bio-energetic Health and "Design Your Destiny" courses. According to the doctors, she should have died before July 2002. Instead, she is in radiant health, feels great, and is using our Bio-energetic Health system to build a very successful life for herself.

I am passionately convinced that we are spiritual beings in a body with infinite potential. I know from my own experience that by accessing this inner power we can truly achieve health, wealth, happiness and success and create the lives we really want.

Helping people accomplish this is my life's mission.

— Rex Johnson

Your Money Blueprint
T. Harv Eker

Whether I'm appearing on radio or television, I'm well-known for making this statement: "Give me five minutes, and I can predict your financial future for the rest of your life."

In a short conversation, I can identify what's called your money and success "blueprint." Each of us has a personal money and success blueprint already ingrained in our subconscious mind. It is this blueprint that will determine your financial destiny.

Your "money blueprint" is simply your pre-set program of relating to money. Your financial blueprint consists of your thoughts, feelings and actions in the arena of money.

How do you get your money blueprint? Your financial blueprint consists primarily of the "programming" you received in the past, especially as a young child. For most people, this would include parents, siblings, friends, authority figures, religious leaders, media and your culture, to name a few.

Now for the "million dollar" question: "What is your current money and success blueprint subconsciously set for?" Are you set for success, for mediocrity or for financial failure? Are you programmed for struggle or ease around money? Are you set for working hard for your money or being in balance? Are you conditioned for having an inconsistent income?

Regardless of how things appear on the outside, everything that happens in your physical reality comes from the "inside." Inconsistent income is nothing more than your subconscious money blueprint at work. Are you set for having a high, moderate or a low income? Are you set for earning $20,000 a year? $60,000? $200,000? Or more?

So how can you tell what setting your personal money and success blueprint is set on? There are several methods, but one of the simplest ways is to look at your results.

Your blueprint is like a thermostat. If the temperature in the room is 72 degrees, chances are good that the thermostat is set for 72 degrees. Is it possible that because the window is open, and it is cold outside, the temperature can drop to 65 degrees? Of course, but what will eventually happen? The thermostat will kick in and bring the temperature back to 72.

The only way to permanently change the temperature in the room is to reset the thermostat. In the same way, the only way to change your level of financial success on a "permanent" basis is to reset your financial thermostat, otherwise known as your money blueprint.

You can try anything and everything else you want. You can develop your skills in business, marketing, sales, negotiations and management. You can become an expert in real estate or the stock market. All of these are tremendous "tools," but in the end, without an inner "toolbox" that is big enough and strong enough for you to create large amounts of money and hold on to it, all the tools in the world will be useless to you.

Your income can only grow to the extent that you do.

Fortunately or unfortunately, your personal money and success blueprint will tend to stay with you for rest of your life – unless you identify and change it. That is exactly what we do in our Millionaire Mind Intensive workshop. At this program, we actually identify your personal money and success blueprint. Using several extremely powerful processes, we can actually change your blueprint right on the spot. This event has transformed the lives of thousands of people, and it can easily change your life too.

For your freedom,

— T. Harv Eker

Unleash the Powerful Promoter Within
Matt Bacak

Dear Friend,

You're ripping me off.

How? You may be thinking, "We just met. How could I possibly have stolen from you?"

The fact is that you have valuable information inside you. You have golden nuggets that can make lives better. Maybe you have already developed them into products, services or seminars. If you do not market your gold, how will anyone know? You must then persuade people to buy and use them because people are overwhelmed with options. But if you don't make your wisdom available, you are hurting me.

I don't care if it's a security alarm, a beauty product, financial services, a business opportunity, or anything else. Your knowledge, product or service could be helping people solve their problems. And if it can't help people, why are you doing it in the first place?

So many times I see people out there and they have the best product in the market. But it's sitting on their shelf in storage or it's still in their heads and they're not telling anyone about it. And at the very same time, their competitors (with less to offer and inferior products) are selling to people and hurting them. Inferiority hurts.

A while back I learned a huge lesson: if you plant bad seeds, you get a bad harvest. Well, it's time to start planting good seeds and lots of them

Because you never shared your unique knowledge and products with me, you ripped me off. Not only did you rip me off, but you ripped off all those you could have shared your message with. Quite possibly, you have ripped off the world! It's your job, your duty to share and persuade people to use your services and products. Discover how to market your products – get them out there!

On top of all that, you ripped yourself off because you're not putting the money you deserve in your own pockets. Change the world, especially your own.

Your friend,

— Matt Bacak

Change Your Script - Change Your Life!
Renee McLaughlin

I love playing the leading lady in my movie, The Life of Renee McLaughlin. The story line I created demonstrates how Renee became the witness of the thought patterns and beliefs that caused her unhappiness. She changed them and changed her life to one of happiness and abundance. While the happily-ever-after ending is predictable, the value of the story is in the telling. I will begin where the plot thickens.

My passion has always been health, nutrition and fitness. Over the years, I studied everything I could find and had even gotten an advanced degree and numerous certifications in these areas. But I had convinced myself that I couldn't make a living sharing this knowledge and following my bliss.

I'm also a "personal growth junkie." I can mouth the words of universal law with the best of the spiritual leaders, and I had used the law to craft many wonderful areas of my life. The one huge gap I couldn't seem to clarify was my work. I'd always had this sense I was supposed to use my unique gifts to serve others but could never clarify what those gifts and work were.

I became obsessed with trying to figure out what I wanted to do. I had learned enough to know you must first learn to "be" and the "doing" will arise from that state. Unfortunately, it isn't something you learn to do intellectually. How was I going to go from my head to my heart?

As I was surfing the Web one day, I found Centerpointe Research Institute. Centerpointe offers a program of high-tech meditation tapes that train your brain waves, enabling them to reach very deep levels of meditation. The testimonials convinced me I had found my answer. I committed myself to using these tapes daily. I've kept my commitment and changed my life!

Meditation enabled me to become the witness of my thought patterns and showed me how these patterns kept me from creating the happiness I craved. I clearly saw a very strong core belief I had. It said I could only be successful, productive and "good" if I worked really hard at a job I didn't enjoy. Therefore, I always chose jobs I didn't enjoy – working and trying to be successful. Not surprisingly, I was neither very successful nor happy.

I remembered having my greatest success at a job I enjoyed and came easily to me. While I got lots of kudos, I never felt proud of that success. Why? I liked this job; it didn't feel like I did anything hard.

When I started to grasp how pervasive this belief has been, I knew I had to change to a more resourceful one that would support my happiness. One day while I was meditating, I entered a deep, silent state. Out of that silence a voice said, "Stop punishing yourself now." It was like a huge weight had been lifted off my shoulders. I had finally given myself permission to pursue my passion!

Once I'd given myself permission, I had a flood of opportunities to use my knowledge in wellness coaching. It was amazing, and I had to work hard not to sabotage myself. When you experience this flow, it's easy to get scared and close down. My meditation practice allowed me to see this fear for what it is and dissipate it.

Instead of closing down, I opened up even wider and the personal and professional rewards have been miraculous.

I now have a thriving wellness and weight management coaching practice. It's an incredible honor to assist other women on their own personal journeys toward health and wholeness.

The moral of my story is, "If something isn't working in your life, see how your thoughts have created the situation and change them! Rewrite your script and give your story a happy ending!"

— Renee McLaughlin

Breaking the Silence
Gregory Scott Reid

During an interview for *Entrepreneur* Magazine Radio, I was asked who had made the greatest impact on my life.

Considering I was there promoting my best-selling project, The Millionaire Mentor, this seemed to be the question of the hour.

The first person who came to mind was my current mentor, David Corbin. I call him "Sensei" because he is the one person who is currently shaping my new career, guiding me step-by-step to create the vision I wish to share with the world – "realizing success by helping others achieve their goals." And more importantly, he tells me what I need to hear, rather than what I wish to hear. He is a true mentor in every sense of the word.

However, the first person who really touched my life, and the story I wish to share with you today, was about a man named Roy. He was my boss as a kid; he was a simple man, with simple words, yet how he used these words changed my life forever.

It was Roy who saw my true potential and asked me a question, which later inspired me to mentor inner city children and help people to attain financial independence in their own lives and then ultimately publish these stories, to share the same wisdoms that he did with me.

He asked, "Greg, you are a real go-getter who will eventually have all the material success one could dream, whether it be the boat, new home, fancy car or what have you, but I ask you this, at the end of the day, what will it all mean and add up to? If I gave you five million dollars right now, so that you could do anything you wanted and live any life you chose, what would you do? If you had the choice, what would you do with you life?"

I remember just sitting there stunned. It seemed like my entire existence was being constantly bombarded by society telling me what I couldn't do or shouldn't do. The thought of what I could do given the opportunity had never entered my mind.

Roy broke the silence by continuing his thought. He said, "You don't need to answer this question right now, or later in the day, the week or even this year. But when you do finally come to this realization, it will strike you in the heart like a bolt of lightning, for this is what one calls their "purpose." Then once you find this purpose, I challenge you to pursue it with everything you have within you. By doing so, you will become one of the very few in this world to truly know the meaning of success."

I leaned in toward him, mesmerized by each word, I remember the sensation that went through me of a big weight being lifted off my shoulders, it was as if I was given a free pass to explore my inner thoughts, dreams and desires and share them with another person without the fear of being judged or ridiculed.

For the next two hours, I sat there spilling my guts, sharing my grandiose daydreams, and ideas for new ideas, inventions, and hopes for love.

It was at that moment, in his little office, I found my purpose. Roy, who was a mere employer the day before, touched a cord within that remains with me to this day.

What is my purpose, you wonder? It is simply this: the student became the teacher, and now I am the Mentor to others, both in business as well as to inner city kids. Sharing with them the same lessons I had learned so many years before, inviting them to open their hearts and minds to the possibilities of what they can do, what they are capable of and invite you, the reader to do the same.

Thanks to my mentor, I found my purpose. Now it's your turn.

"What would you do if I gave you five million dollars?"

Best wishes, and what ever you do...Keep Smilin,'

— Gregory Scott Reid

I am Mad. Are You?
Suzanne Balen

Imagine this – a little girl clutching her safety blanket and her favorite toy. What do you see? A teddy bear or a rag doll perhaps?

No, it's a little leather horse. The little girl and the horse are inseparable.

The years roll by and the little horse lies dusty and forgotten on the toy shelf. The little girl is now a teenager and no longer needs the security of the little leather horse. Her days are busy with friends, boys, school and work. Her nights are filled with dreams of what she will become when she graduates from high school.

Although she has never been fortunate enough to own a real horse, she has a deep-seated longing for one. She dreams of becoming an equine vet helping sick and injured horses. Often, when she falls asleep, she dreams of a beautiful dark horse that she saves. Together they ride the forest trails. The dreams are always vivid – the feel of the horse under her, the sounds of the birds in the forest and the horse's hooves, the early morning mist and sun filtering through the trees. Her fantasy world becomes so important to her that one day she decides to tell her friends about it.

"You are mad," they said, and "Hey, have you ridden your horse today?" becomes their favorite taunt.

The taunts hurt, and eventually, she stopped dreaming. She never became an equine vet.

She grew up, got married, had children and took a "regular" job. The job bored her, but she was good at it. At least, it was a regular pay check; but somewhere deep down there was an underlying feeling of discontent, a feeling there was more to life and somehow she was missing out.

It was at the lowest point in her life when Lucky, a dark black/brown thoroughbred, came into her life. Lucky was skin and bone and destined for the knackery because no one wanted her. She was on her way to becoming pet food. They said she was not safe to ride. Yet, she had the gentlest eyes. She took Lucky from the hands of the horse dealers. "You are mad," they said.

Lucky never let her down. Lucky repaid her kindness with trust, carrying her through some of her most difficult years; but she was only human. Time was her biggest enemy. She always had so much to do and never enough time to do it. She never took the time to read the subtle messages Lucky gave her and, in the end, she let Lucky down.

Lucky had never refused to be saddled or bridled except on that last fateful day. Lucky tried to tell her something was wrong, but she never listened. Beautiful, faithful Lucky gave her all and made that last ride one to remember. She died a couple of days later on a cold and wet mid-winter night. The devastation of such a loss was almost too great to bear.

Lucky's eyes haunted her. They were the last thing she saw as she drifted off to sleep and the first thing she saw as she drifted back into consciousness in the morning. In her dreams they explored the forest trails once more, and she took comfort from the fact that she had at least given Lucky a few good years. In dying, Lucky had given her the greatest gift of all for she had taught her to dream again.

She gave up full time work and started her own business. Her mentors told her she needed a "why" to be successful. They told her she needed to be able to dream and never let go of her dreams because dreams eventually come true.

You see, I was that little girl, and I have finally understood the real meaning of the word mad – Making A Difference.

I represent a company that also falls into the category of "MAD." The company is a world leader in the field of health and wellness. The founder of the company is a man with a vision for he dreams "of a world free from pain and suffering – a world free from disease." It's easy to follow in the footsteps of a man who has turned his dream into reality and in doing so touched the lives of so many people in such a positive way.

There is the potential to earn a very substantial income from the business. However, I have no interest in earning money for money's sake. I have set up a charity and my dream is that it will link and support all the existing horse rescue organizations in Australia and eventually worldwide. I wish to partner with like-minded charitable people – to help them dream, to improve their own financial situation and then to encourage them to Make A Difference in the world in their own unique way. The world could do with people who are mad.

— Suzanne Balen

A Day in April
Leigh Builder

On a day in April about eight years ago, life spoke to me, and I finally listened. "Enough, Leigh," and with that, a 40-year secret and struggle with anxiety, panic and agoraphobia came to an end.

I don't remember ever not being anxious. From childhood on, unexplainable fears overwhelmed me on a daily basis. I knew something was wrong but kept it secret. Whatever "it" was, I just hoped it would go away.

My behavior often baffled family and friends. For no apparent reason, I would become suddenly moody and withdrawn or explosively angry. The more I allowed the fears to control my feelings, the more unpredictable my behavior. Then I learned "the smile." With "the smile" everything looked okay, appeared okay. With "the smile," people would believe all was okay with me, and the fears would go unnoticed.

Keeping the secret safe became a full-time job. No one suspected. I worked hard making sure everything looked fine on the outside. The view from inside was entirely different. Each day was lived in dread.

I sought professional help. The psychiatrists and psychologists I saw immediately placed me on prescription drugs. While I spent much of my time in a docile, complacent fog (what I call "the lost years"), the anxiety remained.

And, it progressed. My symptoms of anxiety actually escalated into severe panic attacks, and eventually, I found myself with full-blown agoraphobia, a condition which restricts its victims to their homes. To compound the problem, I had become dependent on prescription medications. This, for me, was the bottom.

Anxiety robs its victims of all the joy and beauty of living. Because treatment with psychotherapy and medications had not worked for me, I was now at a point of feeling totally helpless, hopeless and defeated. Thankfully, life was about to change and show me that what I had always seen as a curse could become a gift.

For some reason, on that day in April, feeling thoroughly exhausted in mind, body and spirit, I just became very, very still in my misery. "Enough Leigh – there's another way." I heard a small voice, listened, and in that moment my life changed – like a whoosh.

The traditional medical model for anxiety had not worked for me, but what if there really was another way? I felt suddenly awake, alive and compelled to find out. So my search began.

I looked into psychology, philosophy, religion and even physics. I researched extensively and experimented with alternative methods. To my absolute delight and amazement, I found relief. Real relief. I was ecstatic to be finally free. No more medications. No more therapists. No more fear.*

Since that time, I have developed a holistic anxiety management program (mind/body/spirit) in which I teach techniques that neutralize anxiety, without medication. I also found that the skills used to successfully manage anxiety are the same skills that create dramatic positive change in all areas of one's life. My entire world has been completely and wonderfully transformed, and I have the added bonus of being able to help those who suffer as I once did. For me, this is a blessing, a gift.

The damaging power of anxiety has been replaced with a different power, a self-empowerment that is with me now every moment of every day. Joy has replaced fear. Peace has replaced pills. A real smile has replaced the false smile. Even after all these years, I am so thankful to be free to enjoy my life, every day of it, fearlessly, and I am thankful that it just keeps getting better and better.

— Leigh S. Builder

*It is always recommended you seek advice from your doctor before changing or discontinuing your current medical treatment.

Taking the Plunge
Brian Yui

They say the first time is always the hardest: first time at bat, first date, first time jumping off the high-dive. We fear failure, or success, but most of all, we are afraid of committing to the unknown.

I was a commercial real estate executive. Every day, I went to work in a suit and tie, briefcase in hand, and my secret ambitions tucked out of sight. It was a respectable job, but I yearned for something more. For the time I was a teenager, I had quietly nurtured my entrepreneurial drive. Slowly, I began investing in real estate, buying as many fixer-uppers as I could afford. Within a few years, I had completed 15 transactions. I would buy a house, renovate and sell it, sometimes with a week or two. I kept my day job. I was making money, but the process was nerve-racking. The paperwork was overwhelming, and the realtors involved were making as much, or more, than I was without assuming any of the risk.

It was 1999, and the dotcom craze was at its peak. With my other job as a safety net, I co-founded HouseRebate.com, an online discount real estate brokerage. We offered a one percent rebate to homebuyers and deeply discounted commissions to sellers. I envisioned the company to be a pioneer in real estate like Charles Schwab was in the investment brokerage industry. I was not alone. Discount real estate companies were popping up all over the Internet. As dotcom turned to "dot bomb," our competitors fell victim to the flagging economy. I was afraid we were next, and then, real disaster struck.

We had spent most of working capital on website development and marketing. One day, I tried to log-in, and HouseRebate.com was gone. Gone! It was as if my ambitions and the previous years' work building a business had never existed. After much nail-biting and countless frantic calls, I discovered that our domain name, our storefront, our stock in trade expired. It had been purchased by a man named, Emmet Dalton, and he held the key to my future.

As I contemplated giving up, the phrase, "Out of adversity comes greatness," ran on an endless loop in my head. I made lists, calculated risk-reward, held back, pushed forward, but I never fully committed. Losing the website was the catalyst; I was prepared to quit my day job and pay whatever Emmet asked to take back HouseRebate.com. Fear of the unknown be damned. Hold all the cards, Emmet Dayton (may his karmic savings account always yield interest) asked only that we cover his expenses. For less than $100, I secured my future.

I am happy to report that HouseRebate.com has been profitable since 2002. Living life fully is about swinging for the fences and letting go of your fear. It is finding your purpose and becoming passionate about it. Without the passion, you will never feel the full effect from your purpose in life. So, the next time you tentatively in out on the high-dive, toes curled over the edge and hanging on for dear life, take a deep breath and take the plunge. It could change your life.

— Brian Yui

Making Time
JoDee Seneker

Being able to look back on my life and not have any regrets about how I spent my time or with whom is a wonderful feeling.

I was fortunate to have a very special relationship with my grandma, Millie Morfeld, who I named Grandma Mebee. She was someone who gave me unconditional love and demonstrated that life can be very satisfying even when you don't have material goods.

Every Saturday night I would spend the night with Grandma Mebee. We would watch Lawrence Welk, her favorite show, and Love Boat, my favorite show. Sunday morning, my grandma would wake up early and help me get ready to go to church. She would always send me with a dollar bill for the offering.

Considering my grandma made less than $2 per hour, this was a high percentage of her income. She would stay home and watch the evangelist, Robert Schuler on TV because she didn't think her clothes were nice enough to go to church. But she made sure that I looked very nice for Sunday school.

My grandma gave me the gift of her time and made me a priority. This is something I have carried throughout my life. My grandma was a very important part of my life.

It would have been very easy for me to forget about spending time with my grandma in my teenage years, but since she had made the time for me when I was young, I wanted to make the time for her as I grew into a young woman. I made my grandma a priority in my life. In high school, my boyfriend and I would go to her house for grilled cheese sandwiches and Top Ramen, our favorite lunch.

When I received my driver's license, I would pick her up and take her with me to run all my errands. Since she had never learned to drive, I made a vow that once I got my drivers license I would always take her where she needed to go. For Christmas I loved buying her stylish clothes; she proudly told her friends, "My granddaughter bought me this outfit."

When Grandma Mebee died, I was heartbroken, but I can honesty tell you that I did not have any regrets. My Grandma Mebee knew how much I loved her through my actions.

Many people look back on their life and realize there was an important someone but also realize their actions did not demonstrate their love, most likely because they were sidetracked by unimportant paths.

I was teaching a seminar when a gentleman shared with me that his son was the most important person in his life. He kept telling his son that he was going to take him to a baseball game. He never had the chance because his little boy was hit by a car and died. What a shame – all those hours spent at the office instead of tending to the most important person in his life.

Life is all about choices; you decide how you spend your time. It is my passion to help others discover what is really important to them and make certain they are living that life. Everyone has a purpose in life, and it is my goal to help him or her achieve it.

— JoDee Seneker

Paradise Within--Living aloha wherever you are
Sharon Ro

Aloha from Hawaii!

Nestled between the rugged, breathtaking mountains and the gorgeous ocean is Hawai'i — a place of extraordinary beauty and multicultural traditions. More majestic and powerful than nature's external beauty is the abundance of insight and wisdom found within you, often invisible to the eye but know to the heart. This invisible quality gives insight to inner wisdom no matter where you are.

Here are a few insights I have learned from native Hawaiian elders about how nature and aloha can give heightened perspective to your purpose, passion, and abundance. For living your purpose and passion brings greater abundance.

Our elders teach that in simple times, everyone had a purpose in the community. To them, one of the purposes in life is living aloha, which translates to living a life of loving.

Live with aloha Aloha exists no matter where you are. It is more than a greeting; it is a way of life, coordinating heart and mind. Aloha can create a foundation to live by, to build a life, and world you love. Our late Hawaiian elder, Pilahi Paki, prophesized that aloha would be Hawai'i's gift to the world. Each letter in her definition of "aloha" represents a quality of character to embody:

A   Akahai, meaning kindness expressed with tenderness
L   Lokahi, meaning unity expressed with harmony
O   Olu'olu, meaning agreeable expressed with pleasantness
H   Ha'aha'a meaning humility expressed with modesty
A   Ahonui, meaning patience expressed with perseverance

Hawai'i's last reigning monarch, the late Queen Lili'uokalani, modeled living in graciousness, forgiveness and courage despite of being imprisoned in her own palace as her kingdom was overthrown. She said, "Never cease to act because you fear you may fail," and "To gain wisdom is to hear what is not said, to see what cannot be seen and to know the unknowable, that is aloha. Throw away the trash of anger and disappointment from the garden of your heart, and let only aloha live there."

Receive wisdom from our elders. The late Kumu (beloved teacher) Lydia Hale embodied aloha and taught us to live simply, to relax, enjoy and celebrate life with gratitude and passion. Grow "roots" (to anchor you and provide deeper understanding), and "spread your wings" (to life high above to see greater insight, knowingness, and perspective).

Listen to the silence within. Listen to what is not said which speaks louder than words subtly yet powerfully. The late Nana Veary taught us to watch, listen, learn, and be still and silent. "When you really listen, everything has a message...even the rocks, flowers and trees whisper silent wisdom." Let the unknown become known. Do not save what was lost, but discover what was always there including purpose, passion and abundance.

Align with the natural rhythm and timing in life. The late Kahu Abraham Kawaii taught us the significance of rhythm in life, nature and right timing. Align yourself with the natural rhythm of life and go with the flow of the tides, not fight it. Release and let go. There is a right time to take action in life.

Abundance is seeing the paradise within you. Paradise lives within each person and is determined externally or by location. As stunning as Hawai'i is, it is nothing compared to the stunning paradise within you. Paradise is not just a destination but a way of thinking. It is the ability to find abundance in everything and embrace all of life. True abundance is not an external measurement but is what we have within, shared generously with the world (like aloha).

Like an active volcano, powerfully and actively create new life

Live the life you love, and love the life you live from the inside out. Like a volcano, maybe only the tip of your purpose, passion and abundance is visible, but bubbling below the surface, it is ready to flow creating new landscape.

Enjoy your adventurous journey. You may never know all the blessings you bring to the world. Living aloha is like "Paying It Forward," Hawaiian-style and listening to your inner wisdom can support you to live a life you love with greater purpose, passion, and abundance.

Aloha and blessings!

— Sharan Ro

As Dusk Approached
Steve Burgess

Sometimes it takes a tragedy to discover the real meaning of life. Such was the case with my friend, Tony.

Tony was an everyday kind of guy – working hard and doing his best to provide for his family. Tony was a wonderful husband and father, and spending his time with his family.

Tony always had a smile on his face. He would help anyone he met, even a stranger. If he knew you needed help painting your house or fixing your car, he was the first to volunteer. He played on our soccer team but was last player chosen for the team. That didn't bother Tony. He would cheer us on relentlessly. When he did get a few minutes on the field, he played with all his energy and his famous smile.

Tony took a fishing trip with his son and another father and son. They went to a small stream that was only waist deep; so, they could float down as they fished. It was a beautiful day with the sun shining and the wildlife roaming the shores. They caught a few fish and had a picnic. They all told jokes and laughed. It was just the two fathers and their sons sharing a wonderful day.

As dusk approached, Tony and his friend picked out a spot where they could stop the boat. Then it happened. Without warning the boat struck something and flipped, dumping all four of them into the frigid water. The first father found his footing and jumped up gasping for air. He quickly looked around and saw his son, partially submerged. He grabbed him and struggled to catch his breath as he pulled his son to shore.

Tony had also found his footing and came up gasping for air. When Tony looked around, he could not see his son and called his name in desperation. There wasn't a response. Despite the icy cold, he felt his way around the overturned boat to try to find his son, but there was nothing. Tony took a deep breath and dove headfirst under the boat looking for his son, but it was in vain. He came up gasping as the icy water sapped his strength. He wouldn't give up. He dove under again and again but could not find his son. As he came up gasping the final time, little did he know that his son was only feet away, caught by the submerged limb that had overturned the boat.

When I went to their funeral, I was deeply touched by the grief of his wife and daughter. The eulogist told stories about Tony reminding us of his tremendous spirit and sense of humor. We smiled at many of them. Then he said something amazing, "Tony was the richest, most successful man I ever met."

I thought, "Tony wasn't rich." But, the speaker said, "Look around you. This church holds 500, but there are 750 people packed in here and another 250 outside. All of you are here because Tony touched your lives. He gave something to each of you and never asked for anything in return. I cannot think of a better example of success or a person who lived a rich life."

I realized he was right. The greatest purpose any of us can have is to live like Tony, to give to others without reservation, to help others in any way we can. Twenty years later, we still talk about Tony. We remember what he gave to each of us and what he taught us through his life.

He truly was a rich and successful man.

— Steve Burgess

Tummy Tickles and Two-by-Fours
Julie Dittmar

I finally figured it out. I "discovered" my life's purpose! I was taken by surprise because it hadn't happened through classes, books, or all those tapes on "Living Your Passion."

Moving from a career in radio broadcasting to a public relations director, I found myself feeling exceedingly unfulfilled. As my body "disconnected from Source" (as Wayne Dyer says), I struggled with chronic pain and digestive issues. I questioned my destiny.

It was then that a voice popped in to say, "Maybe you could use your voice to heal, to make a difference in the lives of others? Wouldn't that be rewarding?" It was accompanied by this odd tummy tickle–a fluttering of nervousness or excitement, I couldn't tell. I'd later learn that was the knock of intuition at my door.

In those days, I ignored what didn't make sense, or required too much effort to figure out. Instead, I took more classes to "find my mission."

The "knock" was polite; it was the two-by-four that hurt. It came via doctor visits. My body said, "No thanks, I can't move or eat today." I knew I had to create a happier life, or suffer greater consequences.

Despite earning certifications in hypnotherapy, sound healing and the expressive arts, it wasn't until I took the leap from my steady job and opened up my own healing arts practice that things began to change.

People who'd known me for years and complete strangers called my business voicemail and commented on my outgoing message. Their words were eerily the same, "What a great message. I love your voice. You ought to do something with it. Have you ever thought of radio?"

I'd chuckle to myself, "Been there, done that." Then, the tummy tickle again. Suddenly, I put it all together. My training in the healing arts, public relations, marketing, and radio were all connected!

With my intuition as my guide, I founded a multimedia production company and began to produce spoken word guided imagery CDs that deeply, profoundly impacted people's lives beyond what I'd ever imagined. My body healed as I gave myself permission to be wildly successful doing what I love.

Key lessons from my nine-year journey:
- Develop listening skills. Listen to others with discernment but, more importantly, to your own inner wisdom.
- Notice what you hear most often from others. "Your hands are beautiful" (ever thought of being a hand model?), or "Your cooking is incredible," (gourmet or personal chef?), etc. Sometimes we miss the obvious things, or are blocked by our fears. You may not have all the answers—that's okay. Go find someone with your missing pieces.
- Ignore others. Sometimes life calls for this. Be bold. Do what others say are "crazy risks" and accomplish what they say cannot be done.
- Take risks. Go beyond your "comfort zone." Be willing to do what's hard, and watch the rest of your life become super easy.
- Be in your body. Some traditions believe we have physical bodies so our emotions can be felt. And, "If we're not feeling, we're just thinking our lives." Cherish the human experience and our connection to one another.
- Don't go it alone. Find support, companionship and mentors.
- Leave a legacy. My voice goes on to heal beyond the initial recording session; so can yours. What do you have to share with others? Someone is out there right now awaiting your special brand of magic. Give them the gift.

Dare to create a life you absolutely love. Your life is truly a work of art, and you are the artist. What colors will you choose to paint on your canvas? When will your voice be heard?

— Julie Dittmar

Mind Power
Evelina Darlington

"Go to the ant thou sluggard – consider her ways and be wise."
"Except the Lord build the house, they labor in vain that build it."
"The love of money is the root of all evil."
"Be content with such things as you have."

These are some of the injunctions that molded my thinking as I grew up in the little west Indian village of Glamorgan, Tobago. The village did not offer much contentment: small, unpainted houses, a one-room school, a dry goods store with a liquor store attached that stood right in front of the school and church and a "spitting" bridge separating us from the neighboring village. It could be called quaint, perhaps, but hardly inspiring. There was no drive to advance or to economically improve the town – the simple thoughts of a simple child.

Perhaps there was one inspiring thing – the church, the center of activity. Most of all it exposed me to books. The church was always selling books, and my father was always buying (discussing them, too). My father, my mother and their friends often talked about the Children of Israel. Seems they were always disobeying and running away from God. He took away their privileges and gave some of them to us. So, we too could be chosen. I didn't want God to take away my privileges, so I tried to be obedient. I was never sure if I was. I wanted to move forward.

When we had the play "Mordecai and Queen Esther," I didn't want to be an extra; I wanted to be Queen Esther. I wasn't content here.

My incessant reading influenced my young mind. I learned that one of our great Presidents was so poor as a boy that he couldn't afford to buy a slate for his school work. He improvised by burning the back of a wooden shovel and shaved it smooth so he could write on it and used it as a slate. Abe Lincoln was not content, was he considering the ways of the ants?

I was at Colonial Hospital School of Nursing in Trinidad for graduation day. There was thunderous applause as I received "The Princess Mary Nursing Gold Medal," the first from the Island Ward of Tobago. I was thrilled.

Was this a result of seeing myself since age 10, "Be a girl in white for a future that's bright" — a popular nurse recruitment ad? I was thrilled but not content. Lincoln's country kept tugging at my heart. I didn't know then "What the mind can perceive it can achieve," but when my nursing school classmate, Elaine Philinganes, left to join her uncle in Detroit, I could see myself in a Detroit hospital meeting my parents' needs. Call it Mind Power. Call it Prayer Power, or what you will, but that picture of Lincoln's country etched in my mind through all those years was now a reality. Was it coincidence that without even asking (not overtly anyway), Elaine invited me to join her in Detroit? I think not.

Before long, I was studying and then teaching Psychiatric Nursing at Wayne State University. This exposed me to the wonders of the human mind. Later, Psychofeedback, developed by Paul G. Thomas of the Psychofeedback Institute of L.A. provided tools and techniques for my goal-setting seminars. This revealed the scientific process by which the mind converts intense desires into reality. Now, my seminar attendees as well as my daughter Cherryl, her husband Mike, and their daughter Ashley can confidently tap into their own Mind Power as they pursue their desired goals. Of course, you can, too. It really works.

— Evelina Darlington

The Perfect Day
Brent Gregory

My wife and I had seen the positive effects that goal setting has had on the lives of others and decided to incorporate goal setting in creating the life we love. This involves more time with our children, engaging in rewarding activities and establishing an independent, research-based business. In this life, we not only strive to improve human performance through an active personal maintenance plan but also to make a contribution to the advancement of society.

As our goals found their place in our life, I began to appreciate the power of a solid platform, based on passions developed early in life and learnings from our research. My father is highly skilled in the art of hypnosis, using this unique quality to enrich and improve the lives of others. He feels strongly that we have a responsibility to use the gifts we have to help our fellow man.

This left me with two philosophical values that have become passions: the human mind has incredible potential into which we can tap, and society only continues to function effectively as we fulfill our responsibilities to our fellow man.

On the surface, it seems my third passion is numbers. But my passion isn't so much numbers, as it is cause and effect relationships, and numbers summarize components of cause and effect.

These three passions have come together with our research to unlock the practical things that business owners can do to maximize the business's potential. The treasures we have unlocked provided our clients, and ourselves, with structures around which we can build the life that we love.

While these fundamental building blocks are relevant to all of us, they are most beneficial to small business owners seeking the life that they love.

Before we can start our journey, we must decide on our destination by setting goals. Setting our goals provides us with the direction we should go and with the motivation to get us there providing us with a benchmark when making decisions. In the words of Russell Ackoff, "The thing to do with the future is not to forecast it but to create it. The objective of planning is to design a desirable future and invent ways to bring it about." Goal setting is a building block of the foundation in launching the life you love and it is enhanced by a number of other building blocks that include:

A proactive approach is a key tool to harvest the rewards of your goal setting. In this regard, Goethe offers us magic advice, "Whatever you do, or dream you can do, begin it, boldness has a certain magic about it".

A positive attitude, or as F.J. Storey described it in his book, Inside America's 100 Fastest Growing Businesses, "an incurable sense of optimism" is an essential ingredient for success in small business, and I suspect, in life. The reason for this is expressed by Henry Ford's comment, "If you believe you can or you believe you can't, you are probably right." The contribution of a positive attitude also relates to the images you hold in your head. We create our future using things we constantly think about. More powerful, is taking this a step further and employing visualization.

Benchmarking – getting what we measure. It enhances our understanding of the impact even small changes can make, and also directs our attention to our action areas.

Our research has also revealed the benefit of continued development. It not only improves the quality of our work, but also, indirectly, benefits our attitude and its role in enriching our thinking process, as all learning does. A related factor also revealed by our research is the correlation of physical exercise to increased profitability.

Working with successful small businesses has also strengthened our view that actively working to support your community and to help others pays positive dividends.

I read on a desk calendar some advice from John Wooden, "You can't have a perfect day until you help someone that can never repay you." Interestingly, when you help someone that you believe will never be able to repay you; they in fact repay you many times over.

A magic element of our research work with small businesses has been how well the practical application of these findings has directly helped us in our everyday lives.

— Brent Gregory

Dream Your Life Away
Pamela Harper, RN, CCH, CAC

Living on purpose means that you expect your soul mission to be accomplished no matter what the apparent obstacles. Your dreams and desires are the blueprint for your reality. Life becomes a purposeful journey; a means to an end. I discovered this first-hand while working with Steven E on the Wake Up book. Steven E refers to me as the "Queen of Visualization" because we actively visualized his Wake Up Series topping the charts at number one. And of course, it "magically" happened just the way we imagined.

I spent much of my life in conscious escape of other people's reality. Even as a child, I was an incessant daydreamer, imagining a life that was cast in splendor. I believed I would someday rise above my circumstances to achieve fame, fortune and an ideal love. I read enough fairy tales to believe that we are all destined for greatness.

People called me naïve and unrealistic, pointing out that I should settle for a nice man with a job because I would be disappointed if I expected more. They reminded me that my life's purpose was to graduate from college, work hard while juggling children and housework, then hope to retire with a couple of bucks.

I never bought into this view of life, continuing to look at the world through rose-colored glasses. I held out for perfection; to be adored by the man of my dreams in a grand and glorious manner.

My dreams rule my thinking and fuel my choices, particularly with regard to my life purpose. If I abandoned my reason for being, I would surely die.

Whenever I slip away from purposeful living and begin making choices based on a dread of loneliness and poverty, I quickly succumb to some sort of symptom that reminds me that I can never find love and prosperity in the energy of fear and that I am off track and out of balance. Devastating life circumstances flourish whenever I give in to the pressures of performing "as expected." The pain and emptiness is meant to wake me up and force me to surrender to that sacred inner voice, screaming at me to "get back in the light" and to make an impact on human healing.

I must do all I can to make the world a better place. A voice echoes at the deepest levels reminding me to stay focused. It reminds me to lift all of earth's people to a place of health, happiness, prosperity and love.

I withdrew from the problem-oriented doctrine of Western medicine a few years ago to branch out on my own. I worked hard to build a private practice, treating clients with counseling and hypnotherapy until I felt certain that I had a sufficient client base for financial stability.

The day I gave final notice, leaving my last official paying job as a psychiatric nurse, all of my private practice clients called to cancel and my husband was laid off. My first thought was to surrender to the pressure and go back to "work." Instead, I trusted in the fruition of my hopes and dreams.

There was no income in sight. I had to be willing to lose all of my stuff. It would have been so much easier to hop back into the world of guaranteed wage earners and pension plans. The thought of going back to giving drugs instead of inspiring true healing was just too painful to endure. It became necessary that I mind what I still had, not what I could lose. My husband's career quickly bounced back and my calendar filled up. As long as I walk in the direction of my life's purpose, I am abundant.

To live on purpose and do what makes your heart sing requires that you operate from your creative life force. In my practice, I teach people to visualize greatness in their future and assure them that it is guaranteed. The subconscious mind doesn't know the difference between what you want and what you don't want; it only knows to manifest what you are thinking about now.

I was recently reacquainted with a nursing colleague and she asked me a question that to this day solidifies my path. "How did an ordinary nurse and counselor accomplish such success?"

I answered her, "I visualized it just this way."

— Pamela Harper

Imagination Ignites Your Abundance
Martin Wales

Why do some people see their lives full of abundance and others see their lives full of scarcity? Is the gap a material gap, or is it about your mindset? Your abundance begins with your ability to imagine it. By changing your definition and rules for experiencing abundance, you'll more easily and clearly imagine what is possible for your life. Abundance must be a mentality before it is a reality.

Children experience abundance easily and without hesitation. Their innocence and creativity combine to form their natural ability for reaching abundance through imagination. This same childhood ability remains part of your nature too. You just have to reconnect with this powerful mental skill. My kids teach me how to feel and live in abundance every day.

My seven-year old, Andrea, reminds me of the awe and fun in discovery. She loves to learn and investigate through books, play, various media and school. Her insatiable curiosity increases her knowledge and confidence. Using the power and freedom that learning brings, she lives in abundance.

My next teacher, Jennifer, demonstrates pure imagination and joy through her desire to perform. At six years of age, she has danced the most famous ballets to full houses and thunderous applause – all in the space of our kitchen, with the CD player as her accompanying orchestra.

Sadly, we "grow up" and become "professional," while thinking we've learned "enough." How far do we let our imagination take us beyond sterile business mission statements? Has your passion and imagination been dulled, or lost, in monotony? Every day you get up, go to work, get home, watch TV, and sleep. Then repeat. Dance and sing along with your favorite music and you'll feel both playful and imaginative again.

Reaching your abundance mentality begins with imagination. It certainly takes more than imagination, but you won't get anywhere without starting out. And, you won't get far without making the journey fun and enjoyable enough to remain passionate about your goals.

My last child instructor is my four-year old son. Oliver picks up an empty paper towel roll and it becomes a powerful telescope to spy pirate ships on the horizon. The cardboard roll transforms into a sword as we catch the buccaneers on the high seas and board their vessel. That "mission" finished, it changes into a baton to lead a marching band of hundreds through the streets in the largest parade ever to celebrate victory! What a perfect illustration of starting down a path for abundance ignited by imagination.

Get a head start on your path. Recognize the prosperity and advantage you already have. Sense it in every dream, every breath and every relationship. Once you comprehend how prosperous you already are, you'll feel the gratitude and attitude that attract like-minded people and resources needed to mastermind and manifest your own abundance. Connect with those cheerful friends, successful business professionals, passionate lovers, grateful people and proud parents surrounding you. Watch and learn from the children. Even better – get right in there and play with them!

Imagination is your ticket to participate in abundance, but it doesn't do the work for you. You have to take action once you've envisioned the possibilities in your mind's eye and have faith that they're possible. Your abundance begins the moment you harness your imagination for what is possible to *"Wake Up...Live the Life You Love!"*

— Martin Wales

S.T.A.Y.

Jamie Hope

From the time I was a kid, I always wanted to be rich and famous. At 45, I was neither rich nor famous, and I blamed my lack of success on my mom. How immature is that? But I truly believed that she was the cause of my misfortunes.

I've always written songs and stories and acted them out. When I was 18 years-old, I went to New York to study acting. I sang rock and roll in the 1980s while touring military bases in Spain. I've been an extra in movies and have done commercials. I did two tours in Japan, singing with legendary Ohta San. Regardless of what opportunities I was presented, I still did not have fame or fortune and was without my mom's encouragement.

I always wished for more support from my mom. I sent her my song book called, Life's a Soap Opera and I'm in the Suds! She wrote back asking me if I was on drugs. I remember her being a powerful woman. She was a single mother raising four kids. She started selling air time for local radio stations and ended up becoming the first female general manager of a radio station in Hawaii. She was happy and in control until she became ill.

One night I had a dream that I was with her as she expressed her fear of dying. I said, "You don't have to be afraid. You can be free now. You can dance like you always wanted." She died the next day.

Death can make you scream, rant, rave and cry. After experiencing such intense emotions, it can make you rethink life. How silly it is to blame anyone for your life. "You're on your own, kid," is what my brain and mom, told me. I kept screaming back "Why didn't you S.T.A.Y.!" When I finally got quiet, it came to me. Stop Think Appreciate Why, or S.T.A.Y. for short.

When someone is walking away from you, it's really good to scream "S.T.A.Y.! Stop, Think, Appreciate Why!" If you're considering yelling at someone, yell at yourself instead, "S.T.A.Y.!" I find it helps to silently scream this to yourself several times a day.

Now that I've taken responsibility for my life, I have opened a restaurant with my brothers in my mom's honor called Ronnie's Ice Cream Parlor & Restaurant. We used her picture as our logo. The day we were installing a huge mirror with her face on it my little niece ran up to me and said, "Auntie! Auntie! I saw Grandma!"

"Yeah," I said pointing to the mirror.

"Not there, over there," she said as she pointed to the back of the restaurant. I guess mom was checking up on us.

I don't blame her anymore for my life. I can't believe I ever did. Ronnie's is my stage now, and there I'm famous.

When ever I start to lose myself, I scream, "S.T.A.Y.," and it stops me.

— Jamie Hope

The Misfit Tree
David Francis

Several years ago, I had the privilege of co-founding a 600 acre wilderness retreat center. At the time of its purchase, the area had been very heavily logged. In journeying around the property, there was one area of particular devastation. Where once had been a large stand of pine trees, a thirty to forty foot tree now stood alone. This solitary tree possessed a very pronounced and unusual kink in its trunk and looked unlike any pine tree I had ever seen.

In that moment, I found myself imagining it growing up. I imagined, as in the Native American tradition, that the trees could talk and converse with each other. "Poor Misfit Tree," its proud and straight brothers and sisters said, "how sad to be so twisted and kinked. Not like us who stand so tall and straight." They held themselves even more erect and said, "It must be the wish of the Great Spirit that the Misfit Tree exists to reflect back to us how proud and straight we are and cause us not to take our straightness for granted. This service it offers to us." They were at the same time both sorry for it and glad that they were not bent so.

The Misfit Tree sighed in its heartwood and wished it could be like its brothers and sisters, but that was not its destiny. It was born to be different and that was what the Great Spirit of the forest and of the Universe had willed for it.

Over time, it came to love its differences, and it came to know that if it could not develop to be straight and tall, it could grow in other ways that could not be so easily perceived. It found that it loved to put its time and effort into understanding the nature of the forest and all that lived there. It contemplated the living air, water and earth of the planet and the living fire of the sun. In time it came to love its brothers and sisters for being true to their own nature in all their straightness and pride.

Then one day a terrible thing happened. Gangs of men arrived with massive, metal machines. The giant machines let out clouds of poisonous smoke as their huge metal jaws took hold of each proud tree and tore it from the ground. The Misfit Tree trembled as living brothers and sisters became long, lifeless sticks. As one of the machines approached the Misfit Tree, a voice boomed out, "No! Leave that one. We can't make any good planks from that one." And so the machines and the men moved on. By nightfall, all the trees were gone and only the Misfit Tree remained.

Cold and alone, it shivered throughout that first night and the many nights that followed. It missed its companions and pondered what to do, until there came a night when its purpose became clear and inside itself it knew. It began to give of itself in renewed vigor and purpose, its mission clear and defined.

Today, the Misfit Tree still stands but around it now are new saplings with straight trunks and proud bearing, born of the Misfit Tree itself. The tree that was saved because of the difference that set it apart from its brothers and sisters has successfully carried forward the future of the whole tribe and preserved their inheritance.

I often remember and thank the Misfit Tree for helping me to realize how our greatest perceived weaknesses can turn out to be our greatest strengths. The very experiences that we wish had not happened in our lives are often the ones that ultimately offer us the keys to our future.

Like the Misfit Tree, we can surely strive to be our best within the life that we have been given, with its multiple gifts, talents and possibilities. For while we live we have the unique opportunity to bring into the world more of those qualities that are sacred to us in the unique way that only we can.

— David Francis M.A.

The Blessing to Give Back
(Malama Pono in Hawiian)
Cynthia Chu

In the 1970s, I was in my mid 20s and a manager in one of the most technically advanced companies of the time. My income exceeded that of my peers and many people twice my age. I had a housekeeper-nanny and was living affluent life.

During a sunset on the beach, my key salesman and I were looking at a mansion with windows, which appeared to be gold. I told him my life was like that mansion; I had realized my golden windows were merely glass.

After 15 years of success, I submitted my resignation. Initially, the phone rang several times a week with job offers. Then one day, after a year-and-a-half, the phone stopped ringing. My life had gone through a transition; now, I had time to spend with my children.

I started to work with clay—working with my hands – the basics. Manipulating clay was more gratifying without the causality of others. Returning to the workforce, I began to work with the earth and create something from one of the basics in life.

I was exiting one world and entering another, leaving safety and security of the corporate world for an unknown way of life filled with higher risk. I transitioned from being a pragmatic realistic to a meta-physical person, filled with spirituality, magic, mystery and creativity.

For the next few years, I practiced temple work in the midst of everyday life. I lived and learned the principles of body, mind and spirit. I learned from quantum psychologists as well as principles of spiritual strengthening, sound, vibration sound, neurotechnology, audio-visual somatic tools and much more. I traveled to Java to train with masters on resonance and healing.

I learned to yield and listen to Spirit. Following Spirit is like getting caught in the rapids. Follow the flow; say "yes" to what is present rather than fight it. I have been blessed to learn from many masters – wisdom keepers, his holiest the Dalai Lama, kahunas (Hawaiian masters of a specific discipline), and many others. When in their presence, I noticed their peace, joyfulness, humor, integrity, and simple wisdom.

Ironic as it may seem, I found myself helping the local Hawaiians learn more about their culture, wisdom and gifts. Now, I am blessed to open a halau (school) mastery of resonance, vibration and touch a type of lomilomi (Hawaiian bodywork) that has not been publicly taught in 60 years. My grandmother was taught by a kahuna and passed it on.

How little I knew that I was being gifted when I served my elders. I now know I was being given keys to assist with the remembrances of many. What looked mundane and ordinary was not.

The best insights I want to share are:

Be courageous: The root word for courage means "heart", not "strength," as "encourage" means to expand your heart.

Simply live in the moment and the unseen works through you. This is a way of being blessed in the day and in one's life.

Appreciate and Re-nurture yourself: the outflow will naturally benefit others. In these times, don't take things personal, we are all here to give back to what is rightful action.

Your gift is your talent – your passion: seek to find within you your uniqueness. Go to the edge and leap.

The edge of your expansion is your fear. Your doubt is the boundary your own wisdom. Leap into the rediscovery of your true self.

Most of all, love each moment and all those who contributed to this moment of you loving you. You are already a gift of God. How you express your passion is your choice! Live the life you are meant to live in your joyous expression filled with passion. It is the passion of life that fills the world.

— Cynthia Chu

Take the first step
Alex Ngheim

I am a first generation immigrant to America, the youngest of six. My family is Vietnamese, though I was born in Laos. In 1976 my family emigrated to the U.S. after spending a year in a refugee camp in Thailand. To this day, I marvel at how much courage it took my parents to leave everything to come to a foreign land so their children could have a better life.

I suspect many can relate to the story if you look back a generation or two.

Like my fellow college graduates, I immediately went for the safe job in corporate America. After 18 months, I quickly realized I was very unhappy. Then, came the turning point in my life – my decision to quit. With less than $1000 saved, I started a consulting company.

At the time, it was an incredibly risky move. In hindsight, I realize that it is part of a personal philosophy, which I live by – live life with few regrets as possible.

As Mark Twain said, "Twenty years from now, you will be more disappointed by the things you didn't do than by the things you did do. So sail away from the safe harbors…dream." With that in mind, I have focused on building multiple streams of income, passive and active, to allow me to pursue some of my dreams: partnering with people on great ideas, international travel and dancing.

My current projects include WealthAutopilot with the mission to energize and enrich the lives of my customers by providing turnkey systems for building wealth. I strongly believe that financial literacy in our country is abysmally low and many hardships can be avoided if we all have a stronger foundation on financial matters.

My other project is a book on secrets of successful immigrant entrepreneurs. In many ways, entrepreneurs are the unsung heroes of our community because they have found their purpose in being responsible for the vast majority of jobs created.

I think everybody wants to start a business deep down, and I hope this book will inspire many of you to pursue this dream. After all, these business owners usually start with very little (limited funds, limited language skills, etc.), and yet, they manage to persevere to build a thriving business. Surely there is an inspirational lesson in another's perseverance for all of us, including myself.

I am amazed at how many wonderful opportunities I have been given, and I must say that I have been truly blessed in having met generous people throughout my life. I look forward to the day that all of you choose to take the firs step to pursuing your dream.

The first step is no doubt the hardest, but one day, you will wonder why it took you so long to start.

— Alex Nghiem

In Service to the Children
Kay Snow-Davis

You are invited to be alive through the light and the love of the child, the child in you, the child that you parent, the grandchild that you cherish, the unseen child in all Life.

You were born in innocence and pureness and are sustained daily by that power and Presence. All of your life experiences have generated the strength, courage and commitment it takes to live a human life. If your human life was not surrounded by your soul, transmitting life to your heart, relayed by the breath to each cell, you would not be alive.

Aliveness is not an emotion it is an agreement that generates experiences of movement, change and unity with all life. Recall the last time you felt alive. That is the feeling that lives within you awaiting release as your lifestyle. You are not lost, you never have been. The child in you is your aliveness. Did you lose your child? Your child has never lost you and never will. The only way for you to experience "losing your child" is through mental beliefs and illusions that create a sense of separation from your heart and soul. Your heart and soul are the eternal home for your child.

Aliveness is an inside job. You can see it, feel it and experience it in your heart and soul. Aliveness is reflected in all of nature, which is free of the distortion. The human mind, in a moment of amnesia, created the illusion of judgment generating a belief of being separated from the divine order of the universe. When you make an agreement, consciously or unconsciously, being imprisoned by judgment diminishes your aliveness.

You can change your agreement and commit to Aliveness. Now is the moment. You do not need to go anywhere, read any book, see any movie, study to be worthy or "work" to overcome your inadequacies. Just be still. In this moment, gently turn your view inside and feel your heart and give yourself permission to "see" that precious child that awaits your recognition. Be still and feel the love that you are through this child. Receive the love. Embrace your child. Breathe.

When you are ready, slowly turn and face the world, the one that appears outside of your heart. What do you feel? What do you see? From this moment on, united with the child of your heart and soul, your experience of life will never be the same.

In innocence and curiosity, you can now enter the world anew experiencing life at a level of truth. A level that is not available veiled through the illusion of separation, judgment, guilt or shame. Through these innocent eyes you are now viewing life from your heart.

You can see the world as your heart knows it to be. From that perception, you can make choices that are congruent and harmonious with your soul. United with your child, you are the living – expression of love in action.

We are the children – every age, every gender, every nationality, every culture, and every tradition. We are the future."

— Kay Snow-Davis

Visualization
Steven E.

Several years ago, I wrote about visualization in my handbooks called Wake Up. Since then I have visualized and manifested more love, joy and material abundance than I had ever imagined.

Here is a good example of how to visualize from Wake Up. I visualized myself living, before I moved there, on one of the most beautiful beaches in the world, Victoria Beach in Laguna Beach, California, each morning and at bedtime for six months. I clearly visualized myself sitting, looking out, seeing and hearing the ocean waves crashing on the beach. I felt the ocean breeze on my face. I visualized how my dream place looked.

The most important part of visualization is to make sure you feel it. Plant the seeds and know that some day your seeds will become beautiful flowers. Just wait, and let go. There is no reason to dig up the seeds you planted. Make sure you water daily and have faith.

Practice this visualization with your relationships. See yourself with more unconditional love, joy, compassion and everything your heart desires.

Do this: Write down three things you would like to manifest into your life. Carry these goals in your pocket throughout the day, concentrating on them. Feel them being in your life. Feel that they exist in the present moment, in the now. The more you observe and concentrate on your goals, the faster they will come to you.

Manifesting is very simple. It merely takes concentration, patience and letting go.

— Steven E.

Purpose, Passion, Abundance

The Big Ship and the Tug Boat!
Lee Beard

Recently while on a cruise, I was reminded about being told that a tug boat doesn't "whip" the big ships around; it just nudges and nudges until it gets the ship headed in the right direction.

This is a quality of achievement that I have come to call "patient persistence. I seem to be reminded about it constantly. On a greeting card that I was given said, "The key to happiness is having dreams. The key to success is making them come true." It seems that to make your dreams come true, you need to stay involved in the process until the dreams materialize.

For me, this is where being "patiently persistent" has come into play. I have to admit, patience may be a virtue, but it is very seldom one of mine. I can be fairly persistent on a task as long as it has my interest or as long as I see results. Here is where patience paces the persistence on the drive toward a goal.

In thinking about purpose, passion and abundance, it is a realization that you need the passion to stay on purpose to acquire the abundance.

Recently, I had the honor of performing our daughter's wedding ceremony. She and her husband love boats so I used several aquatic illustrations during the service. I used a diving mask to encourage them to keep their focus on God and take out the many distractions of life. To illustrate unity, I used a sail boat figure. It serves as a reminder: just as two people are joined in marriage as one, so two halves of a ship's hull are joined in an interdependent unity; you can't sink just half of a boat. A marriage won't work without both people acting in unity, and a business won't work without each and every person moving in the same direction.

I see our business like a big ship. We're involved in a multifaceted venture and we need to attract lots of people to the "cruise ship" to join in on the abundance and the fun. The success of your project comes from the team member's involvement. For us to develop a huge project such as the Wake Up...Live the Life You Love book series, we have brought on board a fabulous team of authors, speakers and industry leaders from around the world to join us on our voyage.

We would be glad to "share the travel brochure" that might help others learn about this very rewarding information business. With patient persistence, we're all headed in the right direction.

And there's always room for one more on the ship.

— Lee Beard

Author Index

Bacak, Matt...49
#1 Best Selling Author and Mentor
The Powerful Promoter
www.PowerfulPromoter.com

Balen, Susanne 55
Founder
Worldwide "Make A Difference" Foundation Ltd.
4 Brigade Street
Wyee Point
New South Wales 2264
Australia
02-4359-3628 (international 0011-61-2-4359-3628)
0416-049-506 (international +61-416-049-506)
suzanne@madfoundation.com
www.worldwide-mad-foundation.com

Beard, Lee...95
lee@wakeuplive.com
Executive Producer of the best-selling series, *Wake Up...Live the
Life You Love.*

Blom, Elaine 23
800-248-1399
elaine@extremegratitude.com
Author of *A Personal Guide to Living with Loss* (as Elaine Vail),
three more books to be published in 2005; founding member of the
American Holistic Nurses Association; founder of Power Program
for Life: Corporate Wellness -- The Next Generation, based on
principles of empowered personal health behaviors.

Bourassa, Jim 29
2302 Randall Road #242
Carpentersville, IL 60110
jim@jimbourassa.com

Jim D. Bourassa is the President and Co-founder of IFCFinancial, the Executive Director and Founder of the Quantum AetherDynamics Institute, as best-selling author, and an inventor.
www.ifcfinancial.com
www.quantumaetherdynamics.com
www.jimbourassa.com

Brown, Martin...3
Chiropractor Physician, Director
Macomb Chiropractic Centers, P.C.
14300 15 Mile Road
Sterling Heights, MI 48312
(586) 979-6460
Dr. Martin J. Brown has twenty years of profession practice experience in chiropractic health care. He is a graduate of Michigan State University and the Canadian Memorial Chiropractic College. He is also a Certified Chiropractic Sports Physician. He is a very active in his community. He serves as president of the Macomb County Chiropractic Association. He is a founding director of the Sterling Heights Community Heights. He is an officer of the Associate Lodge of the Sterling Heights Fraternal Order of Police. He has been named "Chiropractor of the Year."

Builder, Leigh 59
404-355-3602
leighbuilder@comcast.net
The Builder Source for Positive Change
Anxiety/Stress Management Consultant
Masters in Counseling Psychology and Education
National Board Certified Counselor
Certified Energy Psychology Specialist

Burgess, Steve...69
(949) 831-7136
choose1unique@yahoo.com
www.Ichoose2be.com
Professional speaker, author, coach, and consultant
CEO, Corporate Toolbelt, Inc.

Chu, Cynthia 87
Cynthia is a healing arts practitioner and teacher for many years. She integrates many different healing art modalities including Hawaiian lomilomi massage. Based in Hawai'i, Cynthia travels extensively throughout the world sharing the gifts of healing, well being and wellness, helping transform people's health in life changing, astounding and powerful ways. She heads Spacifica, a Pacific spa-based business that shares principles of wellness based in aloha and Hawaiian ways. Her clientele is vast and varied including many business executives, entertainers, and celebrities.
cynthiabodywisdom@yahoo.com
(808) 330 3793

Deepak, Chopra 7

Darlington, Evelina...73
1720 Lake Shore Crest Dr. Ste. 13
Reston, VA 20190-3243
703-437-0425
edevyd@aol.com
RN, MSN, CS
Founder-Director, Self-Enhancement Services
Audio Tape: *"Systematic Relaxation"*
Seminar: *"Setting Goals for Success Through Psycho Cybernetics"*

Dittmar, Julie...71
P.O. Box 5095
Kent, WA 98064
(253) 639-0770
tellusaboutit@cayenneproductions.com
Cayenne Productions
Author, actress, and international award-winning voiceover talent
Resources for a *Healthy, Joyful Life*
www.cayenneproductions.com

DuCoin, Edward 31
856 304 2800
ed@newedventures.com
Senior Partner

New Edventures Business Services & Groove Motorsports
Business Consultant – Professional Speaker – NASCAR Driver &
Team Owner
www.newedventures.com
www.groovemotorsports.com

Dukes, Jane MacAllister 39
TNM Coaching
PO Box 5
Rye, TN31 7YQ
East Sussex-UK
Tel: +44 1797 229537
e-mail: jane@tnmcoaching.com

Dyer, Wayne 5
Best selling author and lecturer
Author of *Real Magic, Manifesting Your Destiny, Pulling Your Own Strings* and other books.
www.waynedyer.com

Eker, T. Harv..47
1651 Welch Street
North Vancouver, BC Canada, V7P 3G9
604-983-3344
details@peakpotentials.com
www.millionairemind.com/wow.

Francis, David..85
david@dfrancis.com
Lecturer and Author
www.dfrancis.com.

Gaia, Laurelle Shanti 21
laurelle@infinitelight.com
Laurelle Shanti Gaia has been studying, practicing and teaching spiritual healing and wellness techniques for 30 years. She is the founder of the Infinite Light Healing Studies Center in Sedona, Arizona. She is also an international speaker, seminar facilitator and the author of *The Book on Karuna Reiki...Advanced Healing Energy for Our Evolving World* which is available in four languages. She

has also authored, *Be Peace Now... A Course for Peaceweavers,*
and has many articles published in the *Reiki News Magazine,*
Illuminations and other journals. Laurelle is a healer in a California
Pacific Medical Center's a *Nation Institute of Health Funded*
www.infinitelight.com
www.reikiclasses.com

Gregory, Brent 75
brent@growthplan.com.au
Director
Growth Plan Pty Ltd
www.growthplan.com.au

Hansen, Mark Victor...1
Co-author, *Chicken Soup for the Soul;*
author *One Minute Millionaire*
www.markvictorhansen.com

Harper, Pamela 79
866-5pamela
Registered Nurse, Counselor, Hypnotherapist, Motivational Speaker
and maintains a private practice in San Clemente, CA.
www.pamelaharper.com

Harris, Bill 15
800-945-2741
bh@centerpointe.com
Founder and Director of Centerpointe Research Institute.
www.centerpointe.com

Henderson, Dr. R. Winn 19
828-586-0094
drhenderson7@mchsi.com
www.theultimatesecrettohappiness.com
www.shareyourmission.com
Dr. Winn Henderson is a retired medical doctor, author or
coauthor of over 20 books, host of international radio show:
Share Your Mission, founder of The Recovery Group and The
Destiny House.

Wake Up...Live the Life You Love,

Hope, Jamie 83
ronnies002@hawaii.rr.com
www.rrhi.com/ronnies
Jamie's songs are found on *Ohta Sans* CDs and book, available at
Barnes and Nobles and www.fleamarketmusic.com.

Johnson, Rex...43
Rex Johnson, D.N., D.Hom.,D.H.P.,Ph.D.
Holistic Health Practitioner in Dorset, England, UK
Co-founder of *Inner Power Associates* who run Bio-energetic
Health and *Design your Destiny* courses. Co-author of *"Awaken
Your Inner Power", "Creating Confidence"* and *"Decide to Win"*
www.bioenergetichealth.co.uk
www.designyourdestiny.co.uk
email: rex@innerpower.freeserve.co.uk
Telephone: 0044(0)1929-556869
High Tor
Worgret Hill
Wareham
BH20 6AD
UK
rex@innerpower.freeserve.co.uk

Karagiannis, Steve 13
Clarendon Chiropractic Centre
400 Clarendon Street, South Melbourne,
VICTORIA, AUSTRALIA, 3181
Ph: +6139 690 2900
International, country, city codes (011-61-03)

McLaughlin, Renee...51
3812 Glengarry Way
Roswell GA 30075
678-522-8056
walkjoy@bellsouth.net
Master's Degree in Natural Health
ACE-Certified – Lifestyle and Weight Management Consultant
Certified Zone Instructor and T-Tapp Trainer
www.your-health-coach.com

Nations, Kevin 11
He is the *"Six Figure Sales Coach"* and helps companies and sales people reach their highest goals by creating and implementing superior sales strategies. He also works with other coaches and consultants to create a significant income within their own practices. For more information, contact Kevin at www.kevinnations.com or via phone at 877-24-KEVIN

Ngheim, Alex 89
WealthAutopilot accelerates wealth creation for the small business owner and busy professional. *WealthAutopilot* provides hands-on workshops and coaching on real estate investing and Internet marketing. Fore more information on our programs and joint venture opportunities, please contact us at (678)318-1980 or (404) 869-9193 or alex@wealthautopilot.com.
Immigrant Millionaires, a book that focuses on the success secrets of immigrant millionaires.(Coming Soon)

Odmark, Dean..41
Director of Lifestyle Chiropractic
12000 Starcrest, Suite 101
San Antonio, Texas 78247
210-496-1066
twodocs@gvtc.com
www.drodmark.com

Reid, Gregory Scott 53
Living life..."Always Good."
Considered the new *Zig Ziglar* of our time, he touches the lives of his readers by passing along wisdoms taught to him by his Mentors.
"The greatest success we'll know is helping OTHERS succeed and grow."
Living in San Diego, Mr. Reid is a two-time #1 best selling author/speaker and is always available to chat by email:
GregReid@AlwaysGood.com
www.AlwaysGood.com

Ro, Sharan..65
sharanro@yahoo.com

Seneker, JoDee 63
Author of *Making Time for Each Other.*
A couple's guide for Living and Loving.
www.Makingtime.net

Simons, Lyne 35
760 340-6205
Co-Author of the best seller *Wake Up...Live the Life You Love*
Isagenix Crystal Executive
www.Loving.Isagenix.com

Slater, Emily Jane 9
United Kingdom
Carol@loveandlight.fsnet.co.uk

Snow-Davis, Kay 91
Global Family Education, Inc.
Box 60
Kapa'a, Kau'ai, HI 96746
(808) 822-4332
info@globalfamilyeducation.com
She is the author of *Point of Power: A Relationship With Your Soul,*
and the forthcoming book, *Wheel of Life Cycles: The Power of Love
to Heal Our Lives.* She is co-author, with an English astrologer,
Margaret Koolman, of *Gateways to the Soul: Heart of Astrology,* to
be published in 2004.

Sounder, Jase 27
Life Tigers Seminars
"Helping loving people like you create a life of passion and abundance!"
(866) 780-8183
info@lifetigers.com
www.lifetigers.com
Jase is a coach, speaker, hypnotist, and entertainer specializing in
persuasion training, mastery of fear and success training. Would
you like to have Jase speak to your group for free? To find out how
you can now book Jase to speak to your group or present his come-
dy hypnosis show for free, please visit www.lifetigers.com, send an
email to info@lifetigers.com, or call (866) 780-8183.

Steven E 93
stevene@wakeuplive.com
Creator of the number one, best-selling series, *Wake Up...Live the Life You Love.*

Stewart, Jim 25
15 Landskron, Vygeboom Road
Durbanville
Cape Town
South Africa
7550
syncom@global.co.za

Wales, Martin 81
*Y*ou want to increase your abundance and prosperity? If you do, Martin can help you. With his *Customer Catcher™ Systems* and *Programs,* he reveals the hidden resources and opportunities you already have, right at your fingertips, to quickly and easily claim your success in business and life! Martin enjoys his life in Toronto, Canada, with his wife Denise and their three *"Abundance teachers"* - Andrea, Jennifer and Oliver.
Contact him at Martin@CustomerCatcher.com or by calling (416)657-2520.
Get FREE help and information at www.CustomerCatcherTips.com and www.CustomerCatcherRadio.com

Yui, Brian 61
brian@houserebate.com
He co-founded *HouseRebate.com* in 1999, utilizing 15 years of real estate experience to create a full-service online/offline real estate brokerage firm. Prior to obtaining his real estate broker's license, Yui spent five years at *PricewaterhouseCoopers* as a Certified Public Accountant. He holds a M.B.T. degree from the University of Southern California and a B.S. degree from the University of California, Berkeley. In his spare time, Yui enjoys traveling, kayaking, cooking, yoga and performing charity work.
www.houserebate.com

NOTES

NOTES

NOTES

NOTES

NOTES

NOTES

NOTES

NOTES

NOTES

NOTES

NOTES